The Return of the Prodigal Son
Artist: Rembrandt, Harmensz van Rijn
Year: 1669

WHAT PEOPLE ARE SAYING ABOUT
WHY SIN MATTERS:

"Mark McMinn is a prophetic voice in a world where sin is explained away and grace is cheapened. Only by reclaiming the language of sin will we be free to discover the power (and cost) of grace. A book for every person who longs to live fully."
LARRY CRABB, Ph.D., New Way Ministries, author of *The Pressure's Off: There's a New Way to Live*

"Ignatius of Loyola, one of the most grace-laden leaders in Christian history, wrote several years *after* his conversion: 'The most important gift I have received from God during my spiritual journey is to know that I am a sinner.' The closer we come to the Light, the more we see the darkness in ourselves. With uncommon depth Mark McMinn explores the intimate connection between sin and grace. For anyone seeking the profound meaning of the graced life, this masterful book is an indispensable read."
BRENNAN MANNING, author of *A Glimpse of Jesus*

"Therapists often speak of 'invisible elephants in the living room' of their clients' relationships. In this book psychologist Mark McMinn grapples with sin, the most invisible 'elephant' of all in contemporary society. He does so with biblical insight and a wealth of clinical experience, sharing his own and others' stories with a humor, discretion, and grace that avoids being judgmental or voyeuristic. This volume points readers toward a timely recovery of a difficult but essential Christian doctrine."
MARY STEWART VAN LEEUWEN, Ph.D., Professor of Psychology and Resident Scholar at the Center for Christian Women in Leadership, Eastern University, St. Davids, Pennsylvania and author of *My Brother's Keeper: What the Social Sciences Do (and Don't) Tell Us about Masculinity*

"Cheap grace abounds where sin is forgotten. When our sins and our sinfulness get minimized, trivialized, euphemized—when sin is explained away or blamed away—grace loses all its beauty and its potency. But if I have the courage to face and confess the sin in myself—to see and admit that I am, in fact, the chief of sinners—then I am in a place to discover the amazing alchemy of God: that where sin abounds, grace abounds all the more. Mark McMinn's book gives me such courage and leads me to such a discovery. A book about sin, in lesser hands, might be a gloomy proposition, a morbid and languid dissection of our heart's deep darkness. But in Mark's hands, it is as joyful an occasion as a Father running to greet a son he thought lost, even dead. More than this, the book is an invitation to enter the Father's house and join the celebration. It's getting dark out here. Won't you come inside?"

MARK BUCHANAN, pastor of New Life Community Baptist on the West Coast of Canada, author of *Things Unseen: Living in Light of Forever* and *The Holy Wild: Trusting God in Everything*

"Seldom have I read a book that moved me as deeply as Mark McMinn's *Why Sin Matters.* But be warned, don't read this unless you long to be deeply changed, for this book has the power to grip readers' hearts with the life-transforming grace of our Savior God. This is a 'must read' for seminarians, pastors, counselors, and any person pursuing a more passionate relationship with Christ. I believe this book is destined to become a twenty-first-century classic."

SANDRA D. WILSON, Ph.D., seminary professor, speaker, and author of *Released from Shame* and *Into Abba's Arms*

"At the intersection of sin and grace Mark McMinn writes simply, deeply, and thoughtfully in both senses of the word. This book has soul."

CORNELIUS PLANTINGA JR., Ph.D., president of Calvin Theological Seminary, author of *Engaging God's World: A Christian Vision of Faith, Learning, and Living*

"Mark McMinn not only always makes me think but also challenges me to apply truth in my daily life. Seeing my own sinfulness has helped me realize how much I am like everyone else: broken, longing for love, prone to blame, yearning to be understood, self-deceived, desperate for mercy and a grace that is greater than all my sin. Once we see ourselves as sinners, we are free to enjoy God's grace and no longer have to fake it or worry about others' finding out that we are nothing more than redeemed ragamuffins. As you read this book, you will make the wonderful discovery that reclaiming the language of sin will actually free you to luxuriate in the wonders of God's grace and open the door to forgiveness, redemption, and renewed relationships. This is a book you'll want your friends to read."

GARY J. OLIVER, Th.M., Ph.D., executive director of the Center for Marriage and Family Studies and Professor of Psychology and Practical Theology at John Brown University, coauthor of *Raising Sons and Loving It!* and *Good Women Get Angry*

"This book offers a helpful discussion of sin and a hopeful reminder of the healing dynamics of grace. We all long to return home to the loving embrace of our gracious Father, but the first step is—as Mark McMinn reminds us— the recognition of how badly we have messed up in attempting to find our own way and arrange our own fulfillment."

DAVID G. BENNER, Ph.D., C.Psych., Distinguished Professor of Psychology and Spirituality, Psychological Studies Institute (Atlanta), author of *Surrender to Love: Discovering the Heart of Christian Spirituality*

"Some of the stories in this book brought tears to my eyes. Mark McMinn has modeled greater transparency for me, which gives me permission to acknowledge my own struggles and weaknesses. A powerful look at sin and grace."

MARK YARHOUSE, Psy.D., Associate Professor of Psychology, Regent University, coauthor of *Sexual Identity: A Guide to Living in the Time between the Times*

WHY
SIN
MATTERS

WHY SIN MATTERS

*The Surprising Relationship
Between Our Sin and God's Grace*

MARK MCMINN

TYNDALE HOUSE PUBLISHERS, INC.
WHEATON, ILLINOIS

Visit Tyndale's exciting Web site at www.tyndale.com

Why Sin Matters: The Surprising Relationship between God's Grace and Our Sin

Some of the names and details in the illustrations used in this book have been changed to protect the privacy of the people who shared their stories.

Lyrics from Michael Card's "I Will Bring You Home" are used by permission from EMI Christian Music Group.

Designed by Beth Sparkman

Edited by Lynn Vanderzalm

Library of Congress Cataloging-in-Publication Data

McMinn, Mark R.
  Why sin matters : the surprising relationship between God's grace and our sin / Mark R. McMinn.
    p. cm.
Includes bibliographical references.
ISBN 0-8423-8365-4 — ISBN 0-8423-8366-2 (pbk.)
1. Sin.   2. Grace (Theology)   I. Title.
BV4625.M4 2004
241'.3—dc22   2003020523

Printed in the United States of America

10   09   08   07   06   05   04
8   7   6   5   4   3   2   1

IN MEMORY OF

Dr. Arthur P. Rech

and

Mrs. Jean May Rech

FAITHFUL SERVANTS OF CHRIST
AND GENEROUS SUPPORTERS
OF THE WHEATON COLLEGE
DEPARTMENT OF PSYCHOLOGY

CONTENTS

FOREWORD

I meant to pack it. I was heading off on a ten-day fly-fishing trip with some guy friends, and I had packed all my gear with precision and thoughtfulness. What I forgot to consider were the accessories—clothes, food, money, and books. I had intended to take the manuscript for Mark's book, but I forgot it.

The trip is one of my sanity-saving, soul-solidifying journeys, one I've taken for nearly ten years. The trip this year was a disaster. Fires raged near our western Montana retreat. The heat was oppressive, the fishing slow, and the Forest Service deemed it unsafe to both fish and fisher for us to be on the river after noon. In addition, one of the men was late in joining us because he had been in an accident that may have meant surgery for him and then he needed to attend a friend's funeral. Finally he arrived, but only two days later he had to leave again to be with his wife after her mother had emergency brain surgery. Our wait for him had been full of uncertainty; his departure brought deep sadness.

The trip was redemptive, but with a fire-and-ashes delivery, not the wild pleasure of casting, hoping, and laughing through a season of sweet and gentle drifting. But like all times, good or ill, it ended. And we had to return to the weight of life postponed—the period when the vacation fades and reality dawns about all that needs to be done.

On the top of the pile of projects anxiously awaiting my return was *Why Sin Matters*. I was not thrilled at the prospect of reading a book about sin. I already felt petty, irritated, and depressed. I was overwhelmed by what I needed to do and the demands of what awaits for the fall academic schedule.

But as I read, and read more, I wept. I was utterly surprised by my response. I've long respected the brilliant thinking of Mark McMinn. I've read articles and his amazing book *Psychology, Theology, and Spirituality in Christian Counseling.* I've heard him teach and been offered more than ample wisdom and kindness through his passionate voice. But I had not been prepared to be drawn into the arms of our fiercely gracious God. I don't know why I was so surprised. It may be that I was reading the work as a task, a responsibility—one of many. Or even more likely, I read with little thought about my own sin or need for grace. I read with a heart more troubled by a banged-up fishing trip than with a heart open to considering eternal matters.

Perhaps you are in a similar state—more aware that life is not what you want it to be than terribly concerned about your part in darkening the world. We are all aware of the horror of sin and its devastation, but we're less apt to take seriously our own part.

I braced myself for the jerk back to reality and the acknowledgment that I fall far short of the glory of God. What I read instead was a compelling and gentle exposure of my heart and the glorious offer of entering the embrace of my Father.

Mark does not rub our nose in sin or trivialize it as merely a list of behavioral dos and don'ts. He does not minimize sin on the basis of our past harm, biological complexity, or relational disappointment. He is honest and hopeful.

I read and wept, and oddly I laughed. What I find most amazing is that an honest appraisal of our condition brings the heart to new parameters of hope. If I can be so small as to pout over a less than ideal vacation, then what else is my heart unwilling to face? Mark McMinn nudged me to see my heart in the context of the overwhelming pursuit of Jesus. If I make light of sin, by necessity I will be unimpressed with the work of the Cross. If on the other hand, I look deeply into the squalor of my sin, what I finally see is not darkness but the aching eyes of our passionate God, who conquered sin and invites me to dine with him. It is as the poet said, "He built his tent in the place of excrement."

What I found, and believe you will as well, is a dose of honesty that flooded me with the holy love of God for sinners. Grace is sweeter and the losses of life, no matter how small or large, are less consuming as I respond to God's compelling invitation to rest in his love.

This labor of love will change your life. Read, weep, and laugh—for the good news is deeply planted in each page of this book.

Dan B. Allender, Ph.D.
President, Mars Hill Graduate School

ACKNOWLEDGMENTS

It seems strange to have my name listed alone on the front cover of this book when so many other people have contributed to what is inside the cover. Jeff Crosby read a talk I gave to the Christian Association of Psychological Studies and encouraged me to develop the ideas into a book. I am grateful for his encouragement, his understanding of the publishing world, and his friendship.

I am also thankful for the leaders at Wheaton College who support faculty through the sabbatical program. Effective books come from meaningful reflection; the time away from my normal teaching and mentoring activities allowed me to ponder big ideas.

My wife, Lisa McMinn, is a sociologist on the Wheaton College faculty, and we were fortunate enough to arrange sabbaticals in the same semester. We traveled to some wonderful parts of the world with our laptop computers, each writing books and each spending time reading and critiquing one another's work. She is a gifted thinker and writer, and I am grateful for her input.

Mrs. Jean May Rech passed away just before this book was published. Jean and her husband, the late Dr. Arthur P. Rech, gave generously to the Wheaton College Psychology Department. As holder of the endowed chair position they established, I am privileged to work with outstanding colleagues and doctoral students in finding ways to put psychology in service to the church. I trust this book reflects my love for the church and Christian theology as well as my training in psychology.

The decision to write this book came in a Russian art museum. Without the inspiring work of the late Henri J. M. Nouwen, I never would have ended up in the Rembrandt Room of the State Hermitage Museum. I am grateful for Reverend Charles Busch, a close personal friend of Nouwen, who was willing to share Nouwen stories over an extended lunch as I was writing this book, and for my father, Gordon McMinn, who arranged the luncheon.

Some bold people allowed me to tell their stories in this book. I have changed their names and some details to allow for their privacy, and I will not spoil that by naming them here. I express my deepest appreciation for their humility, courage, and openness. Their stories of sin and grace flooded my heart with sorrow and gratitude.

Dan Allender—a man who has inspired and encouraged me through his writing and speaking—took time from his busy schedule as president of Mars Hill Graduate School to read and reflect on this book. As I read the foreword he penned, I sensed immediately that he understands me and the message I am trying to convey in *Why Sin Matters*. This is not just a book for the head, it is also written from and for the human heart. I hope others will follow Dan's lead in reading this book, giving themselves permission to weep and laugh as they read.

This is my second book with Tyndale House Publishers. Both experiences have been tremendous, primarily because of the work and encouragement of Lynn Vanderzalm and Ken Petersen. Ken has believed in me as a writer, sometimes demonstrating more confidence in my writing than I myself can muster. Lynn is an amazing editor. She actually knows all the rules about where to put commas and semicolons, which restores my sense of order in the universe (because I have never been able to learn the rules). But she also engages me in the intellectual substance of my writing—helping me to think better when my ideas are sloppy or my words imprecise—and she does it with such patience and kindness.

ONE

$\left\{ \textit{Moments} \right\}$

Most of life is lived in routine. We have bills to pay, money to earn, children to raise, chores to complete, and hobbies to pursue. Days fade into weeks, and months speed by as one year blurs with the next; we peel off a page of the daily calendar and find a decade has past. The routines of life are good and provide much evidence of blessing and common grace.[1]

Thankfully, life is also punctuated and slowed down by extraordinary moments of insight. It may be a sunset, a symphony, a spiritual awakening, the surprise of unexpected friendship, stunning art, a worship experience, or seeing something new in the eyes of a loved one you have looked at ten thousand times before. These markers remind us that we are more than silicon chips churning out the tasks of existence, but are full of life—ensouled, organic beings longing for meaning, enjoying music, cherishing beauty, and yearning for love.

Of course, epiphanies need routine as much as routine needs epiphanies. Without the steady, plodding motion of routine our moments of insight would merely be an experiential roller coaster tossing us through the tumults of life. Without the moments of insight, our routines would become black-and-white, suffocating and deadening.

Most books emerge from the routines of life as writers sit down each day and diligently produce several pages of prose, and as the days fade into months the manuscript evolves into something good: a work of art, a scholarly treatise, a guide for successful living, or a chilling mystery. But when you sit and talk with the author, you will almost always discover that a moment of insight has motivated the routine. Without the epiphany, the routine would be empty. Without the routine, the epiphany would not find its way into the pages of a new book.

I have spent a good deal of my adult life trying to understand grace. Most of this has been through the routines of life—marriage, studying, prayer, parenting, worship, reading, and friendship. Many years ago I devoted some of my routine to writing a book about grace. No one has seen or heard of the book since, and though I have quite a knack for authoring books that no one ever hears of, there is a good explanation in this case. The book was never published. I sent my two-hundred-fifty-page manuscript to several different publishers, and each of them responded with a permutation of the standard "thanks, but no thanks" letter.

Fifteen years later, I am grateful that book was never published. It was a book produced by an overachieving young assistant professor who was committed to routine but had not yet had enough moments of insight to write about grace. It was a book written before I began to grasp the depth of brokenness and sin in our world and in my own heart. Understanding grace cannot be done without understanding sin. Sometimes I ponder what that unpublished book, with its anemic view of grace, would have been titled if it had been published. Perhaps, *Grace Lite* or *Grace: Because I'm Worth It* or *Grace: I'm Good Enough, I'm Smart Enough, and Doggone It, People Like Me*.

In the intervening fifteen years I have continued to experience occasional punctuating moments—windows of insight—that have brought fresh glimpses of grace. They are not altogether pleasant moments because they are always accompanied with a weighty, breath-stealing awareness of my sin and my desperate need for forgiveness. But they are motivating. It is the second of two such punctuating moments that finally gave me the courage to write this book.

The first occurred some years ago as I began to read Henri J. M. Nouwen's writings on the spiritual life. It fascinated me that Nouwen

> *Understanding grace cannot be done without understanding sin.*

was trained in both psychology and theology, and I was intrigued by his choice to leave the ivory towers of an Ivy League faculty position to pastor and serve underprivileged people at the L'Arche Daybreak community in Toronto. I read many of his books, soaking in his earthy spirituality, his disclosure of genuine struggle, and his passion for God. After a public speaking event in which I had referred to Nouwen, someone in the audience approached me and asked if I had read Nouwen's book *The Return of the Prodigal Son*. I had not, but the next day I found the book and began reading. That book, which I have now read several times, provided a moment of insight.

Before writing *The Return of the Prodigal Son*, Nouwen spent two days in July of 1986 at the State Hermitage Museum in St. Petersburg, Russia, studying Rembrandt's painting by the same title. Nouwen describes the experience in detail: gaining admittance through a side door because of the kindness of a friend, hassling with a Soviet guard about whether he could move a red velvet chair to get a better view of the painting, studying the light streaming across the painting at various times throughout the day, and being almost mesmerized by the power of Rembrandt's portrayal. Nouwen writes: "Everything comes together here: Rembrandt's story, humanity's story, and God's story. Time and eternity intersect; approaching death and everlasting life touch each other; sin and forgiveness embrace."[2] I was captured by Nouwen's story and his book. He was right—sin and forgiveness were embracing. The father's lavish mercy could not be understood without the story of the son's outlandish rebellion and rejection of the father. This was not just a book to me, not just a part of my reading routine. It was a moment.

> *The father's lavish mercy could not be understood without the story of the son's outlandish rebellion and rejection of the father.*

Moments like this change us. During the past five years I have rarely given a talk without mentioning Nouwen's book and Rembrandt's painting. I found the Hermitage Web site, downloaded a small print of the painting, and made it part of various PowerPoint files for the talks I have been invited to give. My wife, Lisa, who knows me by heart, ordered a print of the Rembrandt painting, had it framed, and gave it to me for a Christmas gift. When I opened it, I cried. Then I went and hung it in my home office where I spend time looking at it almost every day.

This is not just a painting crafted by an old man in 1669; it is the story of my life and yours. It is a story first told by Jesus and recorded in Luke 15. This is a story of sin and grace—a story about the healing of a broken relationship—and it seems at times to be the only story worth telling.

The second moment of insight occurred at the State Hermitage Museum sixteen years after Nouwen had seen the Rembrandt painting there. In early July 2002 Vitaliy Voytenko, a doctoral student, and I traveled to Kiev, Ukraine, to colead a seminar for pastors. On that trip Vitaliy and I had the opportunity to go to Saint Petersburg to visit the Hermitage. Tickets were three hundred rubles (about ten U.S.

dollars), but the travel agent had warned me that I should be sure to have the tickets in advance. Desperate to see the painting, I agreed to pay seven times the normal rate to be assured of admission. The travel agent also mentioned something about a tour guide, but my mind was elsewhere, so I did not think much more about the suggestion.

Vitaliy and I arrived in St. Petersburg on a Friday, took a life-threatening taxi ride to the hotel, had dinner at the Literary Café, and then walked along the Neva River as I anticipated the events of the next day—a day that I had looked forward to for so long. Before retiring that night, I received a call from the Hermitage tour guide who asked us to meet her in the hotel lobby at ten o'clock the next morning. I envisioned being part of a large tour group and wondered how I might politely excuse myself from the tour in order to spend time with the one painting I had come to see. But when Saturday morning came, I discovered that the tour group consisted of only Vitaliy and me. Our personal tour guide drove us past the long lines waiting at the Hermitage and walked us to the front door with no wait. I was reminded of Nouwen's story, how he had been ushered past a mile-long line and had been taken directly to the painting. After a few moments of guilt for not having waited in line like everyone else, I relaxed into a calm awareness that this was God's blessing.

The Return of the Prodigal Son is the first painting a person encounters when entering the Hermitage's Rembrandt Room, where twenty-three original Rembrandt paintings are displayed.[3] It is an enormous and glorious painting, eight feet high and six feet wide. Nested in an ornate gilt frame, it hangs on its own light green wall with no other paintings competing for attention. I spotted the red velvet chairs that Nouwen had sat in and saw the window from which light enters the room, streaming across the faces of the painting just as Nouwen described. Colors leapt off the canvas, and I was instantly overwhelmed with the reality of what

I was viewing. "Thank you" was all I could utter to the tour guide as tears welled in my eyes and a lump of gratitude obstructed my throat. She and Vitaliy left me alone as they toured other parts of the Hermitage collection.

For the first fifteen minutes almost no tour groups came through the hall, which allowed me to view the painting intently and quietly. After that, groups of various languages wandered in and out. For most of that time I sat in one of the red velvet chairs that allowed full vision of the painting. The vivid detail in the original painting is stunning: the person in the distant background, the dulled hands of everyone except the father, the sandal lying next to the travel-weary foot, the small sword hanging from the belt of the prodigal, and the brilliant material of the father's cloak. But I was most intrigued by the light.

It is as if light emanates from the father, streaming across the veiled scowl of the older brother, dancing along the floor where the prodigal kneels, and revealing the father's hands and face. Most of the guides mentioned the hands, and they are amazing: the rugged, masculine left hand and the nurturing, feminine right hand. But I found myself even more drawn to the father's face. It is a face of complex emotion. Yes, of course there is relief and joy, but not the kind of joy that is captured with a smile. It is joy embedded in a countenance of sorrow, marked with years of wondering and waiting. He is an old man, and life has been hard. He has struggled and grieved and wept. He has not often spoken of the pain that has been like a dagger buried deep in his soul, but it is a pain that has never departed since the day his son left. His sorrow is etched in his brow and has dimmed his eyes. He is a man acquainted with sorrow.

As the tour groups came and went and guides spoke in dozens of languages, I was left to contemplate the language of loss. I experienced a powerful awareness of God's sorrow over a fallen world, and tears filled my eyes as I glimpsed how my sin has grieved God. Yet nowhere on the father's face was a hint of judgment or criticism.

> *I experienced a powerful awareness of God's sorrow over a fallen world, and tears filled my eyes as I glimpsed how my sin has grieved God.*

Since my flight from St. Petersburg did not leave until Monday morning, I returned on Sunday to the Hermitage, paid my admission fee, and—after a few minutes of peaceful wandering—found the Rembrandt Room. The painting, of course, was still there, where it has been for almost 250 years since being acquired by Catherine the Great. I was the temporary one, leaving the next day for my homeland. The painting, like the story it tells, is both timeless and priceless.

On the second day I noticed more detail. One of the bystanders in the picture—not the one typically identified as the older brother, but the steward a bit further in the background—looks astonished by the events unfolding before him. His left arm is perched on the bench where he sits, indicating that he is leaning in to get a better view. His right hand is over his heart, his lips slightly open as if he is releasing a groan of amazement and wonder. As the older brother watches with a scowl of discontent and a distant heart, the steward leans in to capture the sights and sounds of forgiven sin. One person resists grace; the other yearns to see it closely. One resists restored relationship; the other yearns for it.

As I studied the painting, I remembered how Nouwen describes that artists of Rembrandt's day often combined the New Testament story of the Prodigal Son and the nearby story of the tax collector and the self-righteous religious leader in the temple.[4] In the latter story the religious leader prays smugly, "I thank you, God, that I am not a sinner like everyone else, especially like that tax collector over there! For I never cheat, I don't sin, I don't commit adultery, I fast twice a week, and I give you a tenth of my income."[5] The tax collector does not even dare to raise his eyes to heaven, but beats his chest and cries out, "O God, be merciful to me, for I am a sinner."[6]

I wondered if perhaps Rembrandt placed the older brother—still out in the fields in the biblical story—as a featured character in this painting in order to tell two stories at once. Maybe Rembrandt painted a double feature. The story of the Prodigal Son is, of course, the main feature. But the other story—woven subtly onto the canvas as only an artistic master can do—reminds me of the cost of pride and the freedom of humility.

I thought about my own heart. Will I admit my sin and my need for mercy, yearning for grace, like the steward and the tax collector? Or will I stand in aloof judgment, like the older brother and the religious leader? Which will I choose: Door Number 1 or Door Number 2? One opens to a life of grace and gratitude and restored relationship, the other to pride and resentment and alienation.

I reflected on the many times I have resisted grace by denying my sinful state, focusing on whatever good deeds I can muster, and rehearsing the list of "big sins" I have managed to avoid. Yet I yearn to see grace clearly—to lean in, acknowledge my need, and look closely at God's redemptive embrace that covers all my sinfulness. The older brother, like the Pharisee praying in the temple, is pushing away the possibility of mercy by focusing on his good behavior. The steward in the background, like the tax collector, is leaning in to get a better glimpse of the grace that covers the vastness of our sin.

My eyes fixed on the prodigal, then the older brother, then the steward. Which man was I most like? Whose heart did mine reflect?

Then the music started. It began in the recesses of my mind, and soon it could not be contained internally. I began humming and then singing quietly. A few people looked at me strangely, but for the most part they didn't complain. I sang the words over and over again:

> *O to grace how great a debtor*
> *Daily I'm constrained to be!*
> *Let Thy goodness, like a fetter,*
> *Bind my wandering heart to Thee.*
> *Prone to wander, Lord, I feel it,*
> *Prone to leave the God I love;*
> *Here's my heart, O take and seal it;*
> *Seal it for Thy courts above.*[7]

After the hours in the museum that Saturday and Sunday, I knew it was time to say good-bye to this punctuating moment—

a moment of grace—in my life. I also knew that my time in the Hermitage, hanging out with a 333-year-old painting, had given me the momentum and courage I needed to begin writing this book, which I have pondered for a long time.

PART ONE

THE STORY
OF SIN

TWO

{ *Prelude to Grace* }

In Rembrandt's painting *The Return of the Prodigal Son,* the prodigal kneels before the forgiving father in a state of emotional, financial, and relational destitution. He has wasted his money, lost his innocence, spent his freedom on foolishness, and falls helpless before his father. His shoes are torn, his garment soiled, and his confidence gone. This is not just a story of grace; it is first a story of utter brokenness and undeniable sin.

In the son, we see ourselves. Tattered by the journey of life, wounded by our own sin and the sin of others, soiled by experiences we should never have pursued, haunted by habits we have acquired, we fall helpless before our merciful heavenly Father. Homecoming is possible only after we discover that we have wandered off and are now living in a distant land, estranged from those who love us. Recognizing our sin is the prelude to grace.

Sin is not a popular word. Perhaps it evokes images of angry fundamentalist preachers who seem more intent on condemning and judging than searching for forgiveness and grace. Maybe the word has been used to manipulate and coerce you to behave more like someone wants you to behave. Or possibly the word *sin* has been the topic of lighthearted joking and has lost its gravity. Only as we move beyond these distorted views of sin can we reclaim it as an essential vocabulary—one that opens the possibility of forgive-ness, redemption, and renewed relationships. When coupled with a theology of grace, sin is a source of great hope. In her fine book *Speaking of Sin,* Barbara Brown Taylor—college professor and Episcopal priest—suggests sin is our only hope.[1]

I recall once sitting in a small group with a young woman who had recently had a spiritual awakening. She described her childhood in a home where self-esteem was the primary virtue. Her parents taught her that she was delightful, talented, good-hearted, intelli-gent, and witty. Having spent several months in a small group with her, I tended to agree with her parents—she was the kind of young woman that anyone would love to have as a daughter. But as she talked about her spiritual awaken-ing, she acknowledged that some-thing important was missing from

> When coupled with a theology of grace, sin is a source of great hope.

her incubator of childhood self-esteem. Somehow, deep down, she always knew that she was not quite as great as her parents thought she was. She knew there was an intrinsic need for healing, an inner darkness, a moral decay, which was also part of her character. As she ventured into the teenage traps of promiscuity and drugs, she felt like an imposter, as if no one could know about her true self or else they would stop loving her. She didn't need another self-esteem button or sticker to wear around the house. What she longed for was authentic awareness of her good and bad qualities, and love that was big enough to embrace her regardless of her sin. When she turned to God as a young adult, she found what she had been longing for—One who knew every dark corner of her soul and still believed her to be worthy of love, forgiveness, acceptance, and grace. Self-esteem and positive self-talk could not meet her deepest need. A sound theology of sin and grace was her only hope.

When Jesus told the parable on which Rembrandt based his painting, Jesus described the son's speech: "I will go home to my father and say, 'Father, I have sinned against both heaven and you, and I am no longer worthy of being called your son. Please take me on as a hired man.'"[2] I presume this speech reverberated in the son's head all the way home, and with each dusty mile he saw more clearly the evil in his heart: the prideful belief that he could find a better life by pursuing reckless gratification, the selfish request that his father cash in his hard-earned resources, the utter rejection he bestowed upon his father when he wished him dead by asking for an early inheritance, the vain hedonism of idolizing pleasure. By the time he reached home, he saw himself as he truly was: a broken, needy, contrite man reaching out for grace. Acknowledging sin was his only hope.

> *What she longed for was authentic awareness of her good and bad qualities, and love that was big enough to embrace her regardless of her sin.*

We all face times when the fog of self-deception lifts, and like the Prodigal Son we see our needy, sinful state and the brokenness of the world around us. Some would have us label these moments of insight as neurotic or negativistic, but in the story that Jesus told and Rembrandt painted, these are the moments that give rise to experiencing life-giving grace, forgiveness, and redemption.

✦ TELLING THE WHOLE STORY

Sin and grace are part of the same story, and if we leave out either part, we end up with a shallow, life-draining theology. We cannot understand God without understanding our need for God, and we cannot understand our needy condition without first understanding something of God's mercy. Both sides of the story must be told: The prodigal must confess his sin and plead for mercy, and yet he must know something of his father's mercy before he dares admit his sin. Sin needs grace, and true grace can be offered only in the presence of sin.

The risk is in telling only half the story. If we leave grace out of the story, as many Christians have done over the centuries, a healthy passion for righteousness slowly decays into a stifling legalism. Good intentions for holy living give way to excessive rules and empty ritual. We end up trying to earn what can never be earned. Spiritual fervor is measured by lifeless compliance with a set of conventions, many of which have nothing to do with true spirituality.

> *Sin needs grace, and true grace can be offered only in the presence of sin.*

In the New Testament, the apostle Paul warns, "These rules may seem wise because they require strong devotion, humility, and severe bodily discipline. But they have no effect when it comes to conquering a person's evil thoughts and desires. Since you have been raised to new life with Christ, set your sights on the realities of heaven, where Christ sits at God's right hand in the place of honor and power. Let heaven fill your thoughts."[3] The story of sin has no life-giving power unless it is coupled with a story of grace, perfectly consummated when we go home to meet our forgiving God in heaven.

When Jesus told the story of the Prodigal Son, he included an older brother. Conscientious, hardworking, faithful, diligent, this brother understood half the story. He was quick with his finger-pointing accusations toward his younger brother—reminding his father how the prodigal had sinned, squandering his money on prostitutes. And the older brother was right. Half right. He saw his brother's sin but failed to see his own, and thereby he overlooked how desperately we all cling to the hope of mercy.

In crafting this story, why did Jesus add the older brother? We get a clue at the beginning of Luke 15. Jesus told this parable, along with some others, after self-righteous religious teachers confronted him because they were uncomfortable with his hanging out with notorious sinners. Adding the older brother to the story sent a clear message to the religious leaders of his time: Your good deeds and religious zeal and judgmental attitudes tell only half the story.

The smug religious leaders knew half of the story very well. They studied the law and knew the consequences of sin. When they caught two people in the act of adultery, they brought the woman to Jesus and proclaimed that the law required them to put her to death. They tested Jesus, trying to get him to say something incriminating. Instead, Jesus silently contemplated the situation before responding, "All right, stone her. But let those who have never sinned throw the first stones!"[4] After the pharisaical religious leaders slinked away, the woman told Jesus that no one was left to condemn her. Jesus replied, "Neither do I. Go and sin no more."[5] Jesus did not deny the half of the story that the Pharisees told well. Adultery is sin, and Jesus clearly called it sin as he sent this woman away. But he also knew the half of the story that the religious leaders could not grasp. Jesus knew that we all are sinners and that we all need grace.

How sad when we leave grace out of the story. Because I counsel pastors, and pastors have the same human vulnerabilities as the rest of us, I see situations where clergy face personal failure. Sometimes their failures are quite public: congregations are shocked, denominational leaders must make quick decisions, and the pastor's world changes rapidly. Pastors speak of the silence they experience. In the wake of their failure, friends and colleagues fade into the distance without a word. Pastors who have faithfully offered grace to parishioners in crisis often find so little grace when they themselves most need it. I wonder how it might be different if we started with the assumption that all of us—parishioners and pastors, apostates and devout—are sinners longing for grace.

If leaving grace out of the story produces legalism and alienation, leaving sin out of the story robs us of life-giving grace. When we leave sin out of the story, as we often do, our historic theological vocabulary is supplanted by a shallow popularized psychology and we end up with what German theologian Dietrich Bonhoeffer described as cheap grace: "Cheap grace is the deadly enemy of our Church. . . . In such a Church the world finds a cheap covering for its sins; no contrition is required, still less any real desire to be delivered from sin. Cheap grace therefore amounts to a denial of the living Word of God, in fact, a denial of the Incarnation of the Word of God."[6]

True grace cannot be cheap because sin is so costly. God hates sin with a passion that should drive us to our knees in remorse and contrition. When the Old Testament prophet Isaiah saw a vision of God, he was overwhelmed with guilt: "My destruction is sealed, for I am a sinful man and a member of a sinful race."[7] We see the price of sin as nations and families wage war, the strong oppress the weak, and unimaginable hedonism is touted as human freedom. Sin is a "vicious and mortal enemy, an irascible and persistent power."[8] One who can forgive sin of this magnitude is not capable of cheap grace.

People have misinterpreted Bonhoeffer's concept of cheap grace. He was not questioning whether God's love and forgiveness are unconditional—of course they are. But he was challenging teachers who told half the story by separating God's grace from forgiven guilt.[9] With cheap grace we don't see ourselves as sinners but as "OK." Where there are wounds, we see them as the result of bad

> *True grace cannot be cheap because sin is so costly.*

reinforcement patterns or depleted neurotransmitters or poor parenting or a lack of self-esteem or stifled drives for autonomy. When we fail to see that all these things reflect the sinful condition of our world—to which we contribute—we cannot experience the life-giving depth of God's grace. The story of the Prodigal Son devolves into a story of a father who is lenient or has poor boundaries. True, life-giving grace requires a vocabulary of sin.

Grace is popular; sin is offensive. When we emphasize grace without speaking of sin, we turn God into one who gives us a break when we are down and encourages us when we are sad. We domesticate God into one who is merely nice. The story Jesus told of the Prodigal Son is not a nice story. The son dared to do something unthinkable by

> *True, life-giving grace requires a vocabulary of sin.*

asking for his inheritance early. There is no clearer way to say, "I wish you were dead."

These sound like such strong words: *wished him dead.* Didn't the son just take his money and run? No, this is much more than a story about a large bank withdrawal or a fast getaway. Henri Nouwen reveals the magnitude of the offense by explaining prevailing cultural standards at the time Jesus told the story. No one asked for an inheritance early! To do so was not just a lack of manners but the greatest offense that could be uttered. "It is a heartless rejection of the home in which the son was born and nurtured and a break with the most precious tradition carefully upheld by the larger community of which he was a part."[10] The son was saying, "I've been waiting and waiting for you to die, and I just can't wait any longer. Since you're still living, give me my money and set me free." *I wish you were dead.*

When the father complied, the son took half of his father's

resources and left for a faraway land, leaving behind a home mangled with the scars of rejection and division. It was not merely nice for his father to welcome him home some years later, as we might do if a son or daughter returns from a semester abroad. The father acted with amazing grace, reaching beyond the sorrow with which he had awakened each morning and retired each evening, extending forgiveness to one who could never deserve it. This story of grace also needs to be told as a story of sin.

People in the grips of sin used to visit a priest to confess and seek reconciliation. Today we go to the psychotherapist, from whom we learn that our behavior is understandable, the product of our parents' conduct or our spouse's need for control. Or perhaps our behavior is a symptom of a chemical imbalance. We exchange the language of sin for the language of self-help books or pop psychology. We may see sin in others, and our therapists may even help us to do so, but it is much more difficult to see it in ourselves.

As a practicing psychologist, I believe in the value of psychotherapy. It is good to explore parent-child relationships, look for biological explanations, and understand dysfunctional family relationships. But none of these things should dismiss the language of sin. While some repeat the mantra, "I'm OK, you're OK," it is much wiser to conclude, "I'm a mess, you're a mess."[11] We're all caught in the midst of a sinful world that manifests itself in our biology and our close relationships as much as our willful choices. Our greatest hope is going through the long, slow process of understanding our messes, acknowledging our part in the problem, then seeking resolution and restoration.

Seeing ourselves as a mess is countercultural. We are immersed in a popular doctrine of self-esteem. One of the unexamined assumptions of contemporary society is that we should strain to see the best in ourselves. Sin is seen as old-fashioned, just a lingering odor of repressive times that we have now outgrown. We are depressed and anxious and stressed, we are told, because we are not nice enough to ourselves. So we learn to use positive self-talk, to affirm ourselves, to see how others have hurt us without considering how we have hurt others. We trade the language of sin for the inert dialect of self-help books, and in the process we unwittingly abandon the hope that God's love is big enough to embrace unflinching honesty.

> *While some repeat the mantra, "I'm OK, you're OK," it is much wiser to conclude, "I'm a mess, you're a mess."*

Part of our mess is not knowing we are a mess. Perhaps you, like me, have never been convicted of a felony, never committed murder or adultery, and never abused a child. Sometimes we don't feel a pressing need for grace because we do not see our sin as particularly troublesome. We feel good about ourselves, content with our choices, pleased with our lifestyle. All these good choices and blessings should be celebrated as good things, but when we stop and listen—really listen—to the pulse of our souls, we begin to hear the rest of the story. The tattered and frayed edges of relationships remind us all is not well.

When we look closely, we find the truth about ourselves in the wounded eyes of a spouse or the disbelieving sigh of a teenage child or the distance of an estranged friend. Maybe we see our messes in the early morning hours when stresses with loved ones creep into our thoughts and push away the possibility of sleep. Sometimes we see our messes in our secret lives, as we allow shame to wedge between us and those with whom we share our lives.

> *Part of our mess is not knowing we are a mess.*

✈ UNDERSTANDING OUR MESSES

It is not as difficult to see the mess in others' lives as it is to see the mess in our own. When bad things happen, we explain them to ourselves. Most often, we explain things in ways that take blame off ourselves and place it onto others. This is true for the big things in life—such as divorce, crime, war, and disease—and the little nuisances as well. Not long ago I was carrying a cup of hot chocolate up a populated stairway when I tripped and distributed my beverage all over the stairs, the wall, my clothing, and my pride. As I was driving home to change my clothes, I found all sorts of creative explanations for my folly. If that guy behind me hadn't been coming up the stairs so fast, I wouldn't have felt so much pressure to move quickly, and I never would have tripped. If my new shoes didn't have these thick, bulky soles, then I would have kept my footing. If they didn't make the hot chocolate so hot or the paper cups so thin, then I would have concentrated on walking instead of how hot my hand felt. I protect myself from the truth. All these explanations serve as armor to keep me from seeing that I am a klutz—one capable of tripping anywhere at any time. Over time, the truth settled in. No one else can be blamed for the hot chocolate stains on the north stairway wall of the Billy Graham Center at Wheaton College.

It's a trivial example—one that's safe to share in a book—but there are so many other illustrations in my life and yours. Most of us, if we are honest, believe life would be better if those around us would change. Sometimes we are right; others do need to change. Sometimes we deceive ourselves because it is we who need to change. Most of the time it is a combination of both. Others around us are broken, sinful human beings. But so are we.

A dozen years ago I was desperate to blame Lisa for a tense time in our marriage. It took years for me to recognize and confess that my selfishness was at the core of our conflict. And I remember waking up one day and recognizing that I was not as available to my children as I had hoped to be, mostly because I was too captivated by the pressing tasks of my career. Recently I have begun to see how controlling I can be in my work—how much I believe that my way is best and that others always should conform to my ideas and expectations.

Our self-delusions die slowly. It takes time to tell ourselves the truth. We have to sift through all our impulses for self-deception before we can understand our messes and realize that most often we are part of the problem. Several years ago I spent a year in personal therapy. I don't recall every detail from those sessions, but I will always recall one conversation that changed everything. After spending much of our session bemoaning that no one really understands me, that others don't really love me for who I am, that people use my goodwill for their own advantage, I expected the therapist's usual kind, compassionate, reflective response. Perhaps she would look at me and say, "Oh, that sounds so painful, Mark." Or maybe she would say, "I see how much you are longing to feel valued and understood by those you care about." We therapists are trained in this sort of thing.

But she didn't say anything of the sort. She looked me directly in the eye and said, "That sounds like a narcissistic fantasy to me." Ouch! It hurt. I felt misunderstood, and even a bit betrayed. But with time truth seeps down through our layers of self-defense. I didn't know it at the time, but my therapist was calling me a sinner (without ever using the word).

Her stark statement of truth—which I could hear only because of the kindness and mercy she had shown in other sessions—became the turning point of my personal therapy. It helped me see how much I am like everyone else: broken, longing for love, prone to blame, yearning to be understood, self-deceived, desperate for mercy. I wanted my therapist to collude with me in blaming others for the pain in my life. She gave me a much greater gift: a growing awareness of my sinfulness.

Our views of grace are shallow because we have a pallid view of sin. Much of the spiritual life is slow and arduous and painful. The Prodigal Son had a long journey home. With each step he contemplated his sinful condition. His is a story of grace because it is first a story of sin.

✦ THREE VANTAGE POINTS

In this book I look at sin and grace from three perspectives: psychology, theology, and spirituality. Because I am trained as a psychologist—one who studies behavior and mental processes—it is inevitable that I approach the book primarily from this perspective. Psychologists rarely talk about sin these days, so it is surprising how many findings from contemporary scientific psychology can illuminate our understanding of sinful human nature. I have often wished that seminary students were required to take an introductory psychology course—taught from a theistic perspective—to better understand the wonders and brokenness of our human condition. Many people of faith have viewed psychology suspiciously, and some may lament that I am not angry at psychology throughout this book. After all, isn't it psychology that stole away the language of sin and replaced it with some inane vocabulary: inner child, codependency, Oedipus complex, and self-actualization? Contemporary psychology offers a variety of worldviews and resources, ranging from superficial to meaningful, from potentially harmful to profoundly useful. Psychology's theories and research findings need to be evaluated with thoughtful theological reflection, but once the

Our views of grace are shallow because we have a pallid view of sin.

worldview issues are worked out, findings from psychology help us understand ourselves and others.

Though a psychological vantage point will be prominent throughout this book, we cannot get a full picture of sin without also looking at theology and spirituality. In order to distinguish between theology and spirituality, I must digress slightly to explain cognitive-experiential self theory, developed by Seymour Epstein, professor emeritus at the University of Massachusetts. Epstein suggests that we all have two systems, or ways of knowing, that operate simultaneously. One is the cognitive system, which functions by analysis and logic, and the other is the experiential system, which functions more intuitively and is based on the stories and experiences of life. Imagine going to eat at a restaurant, looking at the menu, and trying to decide what to order. The cognitive system will have certain analytical perspectives:

"The stroganoff costs more than the chicken."

"The chicken has fewer grams of fat."

The experiential system will be operating simultaneously but looking at the decision from a "storied" vantage point:

"Oh, the stroganoff here is to die for."

"The chicken here is fine, but nothing like what my grand-mother used to make."

Or imagine looking at a bag of candy. On the front side of the bag, in large letters, you see "M&M's." Which system is activated? The experiential system is engaged as you anticipate the pleasurable taste and perhaps recall previous stories of times when M&M's tasted so very good. Now turn the bag over to the back, where the ingredients and nutritional information are listed. Now which system is activated? The rational system will have to evaluate the caloric content, the various artificial ingredients, and so on.

Jonathan Edwards, the eighteenth-century American theologian, made a similar distinction between understanding and inclination.

Understanding is a cognitive capacity that allows us to "discern, see, and judge things." Inclination is more experiential, allowing us to feel pleasure or displeasure.[12] We think of understanding as residing in one's head and inclination in one's heart. Our head might understand that M&M's are somewhat unhealthy to eat, and yet our heart pulls us toward the vending machine. The distance between the head and the heart often seems much greater than twelve inches.

It's not that one system is good and the other bad—we need both to function. Our heart brings joy, spontaneity, and celebration. Our head brings discernment, analysis, and reason. It is also not the case that men are analytical and women experiential. Both men and women experience both ways of knowing, though certain individuals may emphasize and use one more than the other.

The point of this digression is that theology tends to be our understanding about God—cognitive and intellectual—and spirituality tends to be our inclination toward God—storied, experienced, earthy, and practical. Theology rigorously engages the intellect in understanding the divine, and spirituality meets us where we live and can never be contained in ivory towers. In *A Cry for Mercy,* Henri Nouwen writes: "I often wonder if my knowledge about God has not become my greatest stumbling block to my knowledge of God."[13] He distinguishes between the tough-minded work of theology (knowledge about God) and the tenderhearted journey of spirituality (knowledge of God). Though Nouwen is making the point that too much reliance on the intellectual study of God can injure our personal connection with God, of course we need both. Spirituality

> *Our heart brings joy, spontaneity, and celebration. Our head brings discernment, analysis, and reason.*

without theology puts us on a journey without direction. Theology without spirituality becomes a sterile, impersonal intellectual endeavor.

These are our three vantage points for viewing sin and grace: psychology, theology, and spirituality. Psychology, informed by a Christian worldview, helps us see that sin is not limited to the tyrants, pedophiles, and felons of the world. Each of us is broken, wrestling constantly with pride and defensiveness. Theology is the trump card, providing the most direct and authoritative glimpse of human nature. Spirituality makes it all meaningful, guiding us along the journey as we face the truth about our sinful condition, confess our sin, and fall into the arms of grace.

✦ PACKAGING A MOMENT

Each of us is blessed with moments we wish we could package and keep forever: witnessing a breathtaking view of nature, resting in the arms of a loving partner, welcoming a new child into the world, or enjoying an exotic vacation. So we journal and take pictures and tell stories and assemble scrapbooks in order to remember—to package—those weighty moments.

One of my moments occurred in a St. Petersburg museum. Rembrandt's painting ushered me into a sanctuary of clarity, a sanctuary in which I saw myself as a sinner in the arms of a loving God, and I wanted to live in greater humility as a result. This book is my attempt to package that profound moment. My prayer is that this book will help us to marvel at the wonder of God's grace as we see our sin, to walk humbly with one another, and to remember that a day of homecoming awaits us.

THREE

{ *Grace and the Confession of Sin* }

The story of grace must be told as a story of sin. A young man staggers across an arid desert to get home. Hungry, tired, thirsty, depressed, demoralized, wounded, broke, confused—all he wants is to be home.

Home. Where he used to sit and nurse his anger and dream about the pleasures of life once he acquired his inheritance. Dreamless and penniless now, he is returning home, where he can privately shed tears and mourn his stupidity and begin to build a new identity as his father's servant.

His father sees him coming. What happens next is a blur—running, embracing, forgiving, embracing again, celebrating, reconciling. It is a story about grace because it is a story about a prodigal whose arrogance has expired; he is finally ready to confess his sin.

The prodigal had nothing to offer. It was not, "Father, I've spent much of the money you gave me, but I'm committed to investing wisely what I have left." He spent everything and returned home penniless. He did not say, "Father, I have made some mistakes along the way, but for the most part I have lived with honor and integrity." He had thrown himself away to seek wanton pleasure and returned in a state of moral bankruptcy.

The son had nothing with which to bargain in seeking his father's mercy. All he could hope for—employment, shelter, food—resided within his father's character and not within himself. The young man realized that he did not deserve to be his father's son and that he could never again deserve it: "I am no longer worthy of being called your son. Please take me on as a hired man."[1]

> Sin is bigger than we think, but so is God's grace.

With this backdrop of complete humiliation, we see a picture of God's grace as the father welcomes the prodigal home, insists he wear the finest robe in the house along with new sandals and a ring for his finger, throws an exuberant party, and proclaims: "This son of mine was dead and has now returned to life. He was lost, but now he is found."[2] The prodigal begs to be hired as a servant, but he is welcomed home as a son.

A picture of amazing grace emerges from the hopelessness of one who cannot possibly deserve his father's kindness. Sin is bigger than we think, but so is God's grace.

➔ VIEWING GRACE THROUGH THE LENS OF SIN

God's amazing grace comes into focus only through the lens of our sinfulness. At the beginning of his *Institutes of the Christian Religion,* sixteenth-century Protestant reformer John Calvin states:

> For as there exists in man something like a world of misery, and ever since we were stripped of the divine attire, our naked shame discloses an immense series of disgraceful properties, every man, being stung by the consciousness of his own unhappiness, in this way necessarily obtains at least some knowledge of God. Thus, our feeling of ignorance, vanity,

want, weakness, in short, depravity and corruption, reminds us that in the Lord, and none but He, dwell the true light of wisdom, solid virtue, exuberant goodness. We are accordingly urged by our own evil things to consider the good things of God; and, indeed, we cannot aspire to Him in earnest until we have begun to be displeased with ourselves.[3]

Even as I write this, I struggle with believing it. Am I really as bad as Calvin suggests? Am I really full of an "immense series of disgraceful properties"? Are we really like the prodigal that Jesus described? When I sing "Amazing Grace," I celebrate the first line—"Amazing grace how sweet the sound"—and feel troubled by the second—"that saved a wretch like me." I feel distracted, wondering if this is somehow overstated. Am I really such a wretch? I go through a list in my mind of the good things I have done and the bad things I have avoided. And so I fill myself with pride and rob myself of the grace that restores parched souls.

My struggle reflects how much my worldview has been shaped by contemporary psychological understandings of human nature rather than historic theological understandings. I love the discipline of psychology and believe it has great value in illuminating various aspects of human nature, but it does not provide a good language for understanding myself in relation to God. We must return to theology, time and time again, to understand who we are in the presence of the divine.

We are sinners, infected with a cancer of hard-hearted rebellion. Sin presses on us from all sides: from within as we struggle to harness our sinful selves, from around us as we encounter structural and interpersonal evils in the world, and from beyond us as spiritual forces conspire to destroy God's created order.[4] Sin touches every aspect of our existence and contaminates even the most beautiful gifts of God's creation. Nouwen observed: "It is obvious that our brokenness is often most painfully experienced with respect to our sexuality."[5] In our sexuality we experience deep longings for relationship, to be held and understood, and yet we also know the pain of failure. The ways of the heart are endowed with such great power and raw energy, and yet are so easily misguided.

Several years ago I realized that I needed to confess a matter of sin to someone. I chose a certain friend with whom I regularly had lunch. I recall my anxiety. How would he respond? Would I ruin our friendship by disclosing the evil in my heart? After minutes of internal debate, I took the plunge and confessed a story that needed to be told. He listened, grieved

> We are sinners, infected with a cancer of hardhearted rebellion.

with me, and affirmed his acceptance and care for me. Rather than running away, he suggested we deepen our friendship so that it could be a place of safe mutual vulnerability and accountability. Waves of relief and joy washed over me. I revealed myself as a sinner, and he accepted me in grace. Our friendship became a story of grace, a place where we could confess sin to one another.

But even safe human relationships have limits. It is hard to imagine that we could express every sinful motive, fantasy, word, or action to another human being. Such complete disclosure is not possible, in part because we don't understand ourselves well enough to know the depth of our sin and in part because we live in chronic fear of disapproval and rejection. Herein lies the stunning truth of God's grace. God knows every darkened corner of our existence, every rebellious thought, every distorted passion, every insecurity, every prodigal's venture to a faraway land, and still God chooses to reach out with forgiveness and grace.

✦ KINDNESS, MERCY, AND GRACE

I have had the privilege of team teaching a course with Walter
Elwell during the past six years. Walter is a world-renowned biblical scholar, though I'm not sure he has ever figured that out. He
is a humble and gracious teacher, and has been a great teacher to
me even as we have been teaching together. Recently, he described
the relationship of kindness, mercy, and grace. I begin with the
assumption that we know what kindness is. Mercy is a particular
sort of kindness; mercy is kindness to those who *do not* deserve it.
Grace is a subset of mercy; grace is merciful kindness to those who
cannot deserve it.

We often see kindness in daily interactions. I compliment my
wife for the cheerful, loving way she wakes each morning, and she
tells me later that evening how she appreciates the way I interact
with our children. Perhaps she gives me a back rub before we fall
off to sleep in the evening, and I give her a back rub in the morning. In these examples we make positive exchanges, following the
social contract implicit in all satis-
fying relationships (I'll be nice
to you, and you be nice to me),
and our relationship is likely to
do quite well under these circumstances.[6] This is a relationship
based on mutual kindness.

> God knows every darkened
> corner of our existence,
> every rebellious thought,
> every distorted passion,
> every insecurity . . . and still
> God chooses to reach out
> with forgiveness and grace.

But what if I am particularly
grumpy some day, criticizing Lisa
for the way she drives and parents
and brushes her teeth, and in
response she looks at me and says how glad she is that she married
me. This is more than kindness, more than I deserve. This is
mercy: kindness expressed to one who does not deserve it.

Now fast-forward thirty years into the future. I now have

advanced Alzheimer's disease and struggle with the most basic functions. My personality has changed so that I am suspicious, accusing, and angry. Without constant attention I would be dangerous to myself or others, and I would surely end up lost and alone. My wife continues to show kindness, though she receives little appreciation. Not only do I not deserve her kindness, but I can never again function in a way that makes me worthy of a kind social exchange. She is extending grace: merciful kindness to one who cannot deserve it.

We might think of the prodigal's father as a kind man, and certainly he demonstrated kindness in taking back his son. But he was more than kind because he gave his son more care than was deserved. In this the father demonstrated mercy. But the power of this story goes beyond mercy and kindness—it extends to grace. Not only did the prodigal not deserve the father's kindness, he could have done nothing to earn it back. The son had nothing to offer. He had taken everything he was due and had wasted it on reckless living. Now he was penniless and hopeless, incapable of deserving his father's care. His only resource was what we all long for most: one who loved him and was willing to extend him grace.

Jon and Karen came for counseling in crisis. Believing he had fallen in love with a coworker, Jon had left his wife, telling her that he was starting a new life without her. After a wild, roller-coaster tryst for Jon—and a time of desperate panic and deep loss for Karen—Jon showed up at the front door ready to admit his terrible mistake. His new life wasn't what he had thought it would be, and he wanted to come home. Jon and Karen came to counseling looking for the language of sin and grace.

Jon had sinned. Whatever hope that remained in his marriage with Karen rested in Jon's ability to admit his sin, in his utter inability to deserve Karen's kindness, and in Karen's capacity to extend grace. After many weeks, some tense words, frank confessions, many doubts and tears, and the excruciating work of forgiveness, Jon and Karen reconciled and moved forward with their life together. I recall how imbalanced it all seemed. Jon had nothing to offer other than confession of sin. Karen, so wounded by Jon, writhed in pain until she finally found her place of repose: She extended grace when Jon could do nothing to deserve it.

Jon's only hope to reconcile with Karen was found in his contrition and confession. He needed to look at his sin, confess it as wrong, and plead for the undeserved forgiveness and kindness of his lifelong partner. Without confession he had no chance of reconciliation. Whenever he slipped into self-pity, justifying his sin because Karen had not been adequately attentive or caring or sexually adventurous, he turned away from the possibility of forgiveness, reconciliation, and grace. But when he humbly admitted his sin and took responsibility for what he had done, he allowed Karen to give him the gift of grace he longed for. It was beautiful to watch as Karen also saw ways she had wounded Jon, confessed them, and sought his forgiveness. They went away from counseling holding one another in arms of grace.

If we view God apart from our sin, we may see God's kindness. But only when we apprehend the depth of our transgression and God's abhorrence of sin—that we *do not* and *can never* deserve his kindness—can we really grasp the meaning of grace. In the New Testament the apostle Paul put it this way: "Now, no one is likely to die for a good person, though someone might be willing to die for a person who is especially good. But God showed his great love for us by sending Christ to die for us while we were still sinners."[7]

In the early fifth century Augustine used the phrase *non posse non peccare,* which means that it is not possible for us not to sin. We are wayward prodigals who cannot deserve God's merciful kindness, but in grace God extends kindness nonetheless. Grace resides in God's character and has nothing to do with our capacity to deserve it. The apostle Paul writes, "He is so rich in kindness that he purchased our freedom through the blood of his Son, and our sins are forgiven."[8] God's grace is made evident because of our sin.

→ THREE DIMENSIONS OF SIN

We fail to grasp the extent and gravity of our sin when we see it in one dimension. We sometimes think that if we obey the Ten Commandments or if we at least behave better than today's infamous celebrities—the ones who are arrested or defrocked for public scandals—then sin does not really have such a strong grip on our lives. But sin is bigger and more powerful than we know. Sin engulfs us in three dimensions: *sinfulness, sins,* and the *consequences of sin.*[9]

To illustrate the three dimensions of sin, I turn to what experimental psychologists call *white noise.* White noise is the obnoxious sound of static, like what you might get if you turned up the volume on your stereo and let the dial rest between radio stations. Imagine sitting in a university lab, trying to rearrange scrambled letters to solve an anagram, when loud static suddenly begins in the headphones you are required to wear. To what extent would the static interfere with your problem-solving ability? White noise may not seem that unpleasant from this description, but if it is persistent and loud enough, it can be quite distracting and annoying. Let's say that the white noise generator is connected to a toggle switch with an On and Off position. The On position produces cacophony; the Off renders silence.

> *Sin is bigger and more powerful than we know.*

Sometimes we fall prey to a toggle-switch view of sin: either we are sinning at this moment—the toggle switch is On, and the noise of sin surrounds us—or we are not sinning—the toggle switch is Off, and we are living in a state of purity. Either we are violating

36

God's commandments or we are not. Either we are gossiping or lying or stealing, or we are not. Toggle switch On. Toggle switch Off. The simplicity of a toggle-switch view of sin is compelling, but it underestimates the power of sin.

Sinfulness: The White Noise Is Always On

We live in a world where the white noise of sin is always humming. It can never be turned off completely. We are born as sinful creatures and enter a sinful world even before we have the choice to sin. This *sinfulness* speaks to our natural disposition, a malignant condition that influences the very fabric of creation and touches every aspect of our existence. In the Old Testament, Israel's King David sees this reality: "I was born a sinner—yes, from the moment my mother conceived me."[10] Centuries later Augustine reflected: "For in your sight, no one is free from sin, not even the infant whose life is but a day upon the earth."[11]

We are all bent souls—every one of us—inclined toward both good and evil from the moment we are conceived. It is not possible for us not to sin. Something is fundamentally wrong with us, and it begins before we have conscious choice, and it can never be overcome this side of heaven.

There is no need to feel guilty for this predicament of sinfulness we are in. Theologians call it original sin because it comes with us into life. We did not choose it, and we cannot choose to rid ourselves of it. Sinfulness infects both our thinking and our affections, blinding us to truth and causing our hearts to stray. We are "mired in a desperate and deplorable condition."[12]

> *We are all bent souls—every one of us—inclined toward both good and evil from the moment we are conceived.*

Theologian and seminary professor Millard Erickson writes:

"Many people are unable to grasp the concept of sin. The idea of *sin* as an inner force, an inherent condition, a controlling power, is largely unknown. People today think more in terms of *sins,* that is, individual wrong acts."[13]

Similar assertions can be found throughout the writings of Christian systematic theologians. J. I. Packer notes: "The assertion of original sin makes the point that we are . . . born with a nature enslaved to sin."[14] Donald Bloesch writes: "Sin, in the biblical perspective, is both an act and a state. . . . What should be borne in mind is that the bias of sin precedes the act of sin."[15]

The white noise is always on—from the moment of birth to the moment of death—annoying us, distracting us, causing us to stumble.

When my children were young, they would fall and scrape their knees, as children do. One day I realized something sad about my character. When they fell, I experienced a surge of inner anger. How backward is that? At a moment when they needed my compassion and care, my first inclination was anger. As I thought about it, the white noise began to make some sense. As their father, I believed my job was to protect and care for them. When they fell, it meant that I failed at my job. Rather than changing my belief that I should always be able to protect them, I blamed them for falling and felt angry. All of this simmered beneath the surface. Outwardly, I suppressed my surge of anger and showed them the care and compassion they needed. I raced to their aid, expressed sympathy, and helped care for their wounds. I didn't sin outwardly when they scraped their knees, but my inner state reflected the sinfulness of my character. Each fall and each interior surge of anger reminded me that I am not quite right. Something about me is bent, wrong, distorted, crooked. I am a sinful person even when I do not behave in sin. I can hear the hum of the white noise.

No human experience is completely devoid of sin. We all love people, and that love reflects the most noble and good facets of human nature. But our love is never completely pure. There is always a hint of self-interest or self-absorption. Our hearts cry for justice, and we feel indignant when we see evidence of racism, ageism, sexism, and oppression. But even in the midst of our indignation—which is almost completely good—don't we also catch glimpses of a smug sense of self-righteousness or superiority, especially over those who care less about justice than we do? The white noise is always on. We have become so accustomed to it that we cannot even imagine the freedom of silence.

Sins: Cranking Up the Volume

The cascading crisis of sin begins with our state of original sinfulness, but it does not end there. We choose—consciously and unconsciously—to commit *sins*. We willfully violate God's moral instruction, crank up the volume, and immerse ourselves in the white noise. As sinful creatures we rebel against God in our thoughts, attitudes, and behaviors. We do and think things we should not, and we fail to do and think the things we should. God established rules, and we break them.

Though we may tend to minimize our sins by focusing on worse things that others have done, we are all sinners. The New Testament reminds us: "All have sinned; all fall short of God's glorious standard. Yet now God in his gracious kindness declares us not guilty. He has done this through Christ Jesus, who has freed us by taking away our sins."[16]

This is familiar territory. Life's journey is marked by forks in the road, and sometimes the various paths are clearly marked Right and Wrong. Every day we face new forks, and we choose our path. Sometimes—and we would hope most of the time—we choose the right path, and sometimes we venture the wrong way and rebel against what we know is God's desire. Whether we hold as our standard the Ten Commandments of the Old Testament, the Seven Deadly Sins of the ancient church, or the sermon that Jesus preached on the mount, we see that we don't always live up to standards of proper conduct.[17] Not only are we capable of choosing the wrong path, but we are also prone to do so.

When Nouwen observed that our "brokenness is often most painfully experienced with respect to our sexuality," he was reflecting both our sinfulness and our willful sins.[18] We so easily lust and fantasize about that which is not ours to pursue because our hearts are crooked, broken by the effects of living in a sinful world. The white noise is always on, bombarding us in grocery stores and bookstores, on the Internet and prime-time television, at the park and the beach, complicating our friendships and haunting our marriages. This is what life looks like in our sinful state, and even if we never committed acts of sexual sin, our lives would be plagued by the chronic challenge of sexuality in a broken world.

> *In the midst of the chronic low-level noise of our broken world, we sometimes crank up the volume and choose evil. We commit sins.*

But then, in the midst of the chronic, low-level noise of our broken world, we sometimes crank up the volume and choose evil. We commit sins. One person becomes addicted to Internet porn, another to romance novels. One person commits adultery, another avoids a spouse by deliberately escaping into a world of fantasy, lust, and compulsive masturbation. Searching for beautiful music, we end up deafened by the noise of sinful choices.

The Consequences of Sin: Deafened by a Noisy World

Third, because we are sinners living in a sinful world, we are constantly surrounded by the *consequences of sin*. We are deafened

by our own sin and the sin of others, and our sin contributes to
the deafening of others. If I act sinfully toward my spouse, she will
experience some degree of loss and suffering as the result of my sin.
The abused or abandoned child lives with consequences of sin for
a lifetime. The child of an alcoholic parent finds the world an
unpredictable and dangerous place. Veterans are destined to wheel-
chairs because of the tragedies of war. Alvin Plantinga, a philosopher at the University of Notre Dame, states: "Because of our
social nature, sin and its effects can be like a contagion that spreads
from one to another, eventually corrupting an entire society or
segment of it."[19] Sin is costly.

Jennifer was a bright young woman, newly married, trying
desperately to recover from that awful Wednesday evening.
Finances were tight, as they often are for newlyweds, so Jennifer
took a job at the local convenience store. She stepped away from
the counter one evening to get something from the back room
when she realized that a customer had followed her. The next
moments were a horrifying haze of knife-point threats, partial
disrobing, the foul stench of unwanted closeness, and ultimately
forced sexual penetration. When the rapist was satisfied, he
holstered his knife and walked out the front door as if he had
bought a pack of chewing gum or cigarettes. Meanwhile Jennifer
lay sobbing beside cases of beer in the back room, forever changed.

In our counseling, Jennifer and I needed the language of sin.
How else could such horror be understood? Her perpetrator had
not merely made a mistake. This was not just a bad choice. This
was horrendous sin, and it needed to be named and grieved, over
and over. We needed the language of sin to exonerate her, even as
some people in her life blamed her for the rape. This was not her
doing. It was not her sin. She was targeted, stalked, and devastated
by the sin of another.

Events like this change people. In the months following the

rape, Jennifer found herself irritable, depressed, annoyed easily by her husband. She screamed out in rage and anxiety, but the rapist who caused her pain was not there to hear, so her feelings spilled over onto undeserving loved ones. Her relationships became strained, her emotions frazzled, her hope compromised.

Here we see the complexity of sin. It is not merely packaged inside the skin of a single human being. We are social beings, constantly interacting with one another, always being influenced by the sin of the world around us. Jennifer had been violated, and though she had no culpability for this tragic rape, the rape cost her so dearly that it submerged her into a pattern of sinful and damaging interactions with family members. With time she was able to grieve her loss, recover the majority of her hope, renew strained relationships with family members, and move ahead with life. But it would be false to say she recovered from rape. Humans never fully recover from such trauma.

It is easy to see how Jennifer was wounded by the sin of another, especially such a catastrophic offense. Each of us has been wounded by others' sin, though perhaps not as dramatically. We carry the scars of neglect, taunting, abuse, aggression, rejection, and isolation. Each day we live with the consequences of others' sinful choices.

It is more difficult to see that we also wound others with our sin. With each word of criticism and act of selfishness, we hurt those in our path. With every angry honk on the freeway, every vengeful attitude and action, and every word of gossip, we add to the sin problem. Sin is costly, whether it is others' sin against us or our sin against others.

Whereas there is little point to feeling guilty for our state of sinfulness, guilt is an appropriate response to willful acts of sin and

> *Sin is costly, whether it is others' sin against us or our sin against others.*

the consequences of those sins. Guilt wakes us up, causes us to grieve our wrongdoing, brings us empathic sorrow for those we have hurt, and draws us to a place of confession. Because we have largely lost the language of sin in today's society, we sometimes treat guilt with disdain, as if it is neurotic baggage from a repressive time in human history. Sadly, psychology sometimes undermines healthy guilt, assuming that good mental health means always thinking positive thoughts about oneself.

This trite view of human experience is changing as recent findings in psychology have demonstrated that guilt can have positive implications. A sense of guilt over a specific misdeed is associated with empathy for the pain caused to others.[20] If I hurt you and feel guilty, it will help me understand the pain you are in. In contrast, shame is self-focused and unspecific. Guilt says, "I did something wrong, I hurt you deeply, and I feel terrible about it." Shame says, "I am a bad person and feel terrible about myself." Guilt helps us focus on the other; shame absorbs us in self-pity and self-recrimination. Guilt is an appropriate response to our acts of sin. When we sin, we hurt others and we grieve God. Sin has consequences.

As we contemplate why sin matters, we must consider all three of these dimensions—*sinfulness, sins,* and the *consequences of sin*—and indeed all three are at work in every individual and group. The adult struggling through the agony of past sexual abuse is profoundly aware that things are not right in this broken world *(sinfulness),* wrestles with the compelling desire to ease the pain by reaching out for the temporary comfort found in harmful choices *(sins),* and lives each day with the *consequences* of the perpetrator's sin. All three—sinfulness, sinful choices, and

> As we contemplate why sin matters, we must consider all three of these dimensions— sinfulness, sins, and the consequences of sin.

the consequences of sin—operate continuously in each of our lives and permeate all creation.

→ GLIMPSING GRACE

The point of this synopsis of sin is not that we are as bad as we can be. Of course we are not. The point is that we, as sinful humans, can never be good enough to earn God's kindness. Our sinfulness is bigger than we want to imagine. Only as we begin to grasp the immensity of the sin problem are we able to glimpse the depth of God's grace, and paradoxically, seeing God's grace gives us courage to face our sinfulness.

Some people may avoid a language of sin because it makes them feel small and frail. Nothing could be further from the truth. The honest language of sin prepares us to see our infinite value in the arms of God, to breathe in the fragrance of life-giving love, and then to offer that love lavishly to ourselves and others. Spiritual leader Richard J. Foster reflects: "And so it is. If I know, really know, that God loves me, everything is changed. I am no longer a trifling speck in a meaningless cosmos. I am an eternal creature of infinite worth living in a universe animated by love and care and friendship."[21]

> Only as we begin to grasp the immensity of the sin problem are we able to glimpse the depth of God's grace, and paradoxically, seeing God's grace gives us courage to face our sinfulness.

Our only hope is to fall, like prodigals, before our gracious God, who then lifts us to our feet, clothes us in a spectacular robe, and throws a party in our honor. Yes, our sin is worse than we think. God's response is better than we can possibly imagine.

FOUR

{ *Sin and the Promise of Grace* }

If the story of grace must be told as a story of sin, the converse is also true: The story of sin must be told as a story of grace. Seeing our sinfulness helps us grasp the immensity of God's grace, but we can bear to see our sin only when we anticipate the possibility of grace.

In graduate school I learned to administer various intelligence and personality tests, including tests for preschool children. As I administered a social judgment test to a three-year-old, I asked her what she should do if she broke a toy that belonged to a friend. With great confidence she blurted, "Hide it." I bit my cheek to keep from laughing, while recognizing there is something profoundly honest about her response. Though she lacked the vocabulary to express it, this three-year-old was really saying, "Hide it. Most friends will not be merciful."

Our fears drive us into hiding when we mess up. We need an environment of grace before we are willing to admit our mistakes. I recently witnessed two teenagers run their Honda Civic into another car in a parking lot. It was an accident of inexperience; probably the driver confused the brake with the gas pedal for a moment, resulting in the sickening sound of steel against steel. These two teenagers, fear etched on their faces, looked around quickly to see if anyone had seen. I suspect they both had the same first impulse: to drive off quickly in order to avoid the confrontation and consequences that lay ahead. In their own way they were blurting out, "Hide it. There will be no mercy here." When they saw me, they realized I was a witness, so they stayed put until the driver of the other car came out of the store.

Adults have the same tendency. When hints of public scandals ride network airwaves into our living rooms, they are inevitably followed by denials. "Hide it." We follow the same pattern privately. Our first impulse is to hide our transgressions, cover them up, keep them private. "Hide it. There will be no mercy here." Yet something is woven into the human soul that makes us vaguely unhappy about hiding our sin. Deep down we want to confess, to admit our wrong, to seek reconciliation.

The Prodigal Son had hidden long enough. He reclaimed his longing for reconciliation as he was feeding swine, longing to eat pig slop. The Bible says that "he finally came to his senses."[1] We don't know what caused his sudden insight—perhaps he was hungry or maybe the poverty of loneliness had chilled him to the bone—but he knew what he needed to do. He needed to head home, to confess his sin, and to seek mercy. A subtle mystery is easily missed when first reading this story. Why did the son make the long journey home instead of going somewhere closer by? Why not head to the local synagogue for help, to his pig-farmer boss, or to one of his friends whom he used to party with? Perhaps he tried all of these options, "but no one gave him anything."[2] There was no mercy to be found.

But the young man knew one place of mercy. It was a place he never anticipated going again, a place of bad memories and burned bridges, a place he had disfigured with his foolish pride. But a man of grace lived there, and so the son trudged back across deserts and mountains to confess his sin and be fed. He needed the promise of grace before he dared admit the depth of his sin.

➔ VIEWING SIN THROUGH
THE LENS OF GRACE

In Victor Hugo's masterpiece *Les Miserables,* Jean Valjean is a
hardened and cynical ex-convict looking for a place to spend the
night. Scorned by all the inns in town, he ends up at Monseigneur
Bienvenu's house. Rather than sending Valjean away, the bishop
welcomes the foul-smelling man into his home and provides a
meal, which Valjean scarfs down like an animal. As the priest offers
him a place to sleep, Valjean says with a horrible laugh and a wild
look, "Who tells you that I am not a murderer?"

The bishop replied, "God will take care of that."

After everyone is asleep, Jean Valjean sneaks back into the
kitchen, steals six silver plates, and escapes into the night. Soldiers
see him running, apprehend him, find the silver, and bring him
back to the bishop the following morning. But the bishop, rather
than accuse the man and send him back to prison, goes to the
mantle, collects two silver candlesticks, and hands them to Valjean,
saying: "I gave you the candlesticks also, which are silver like the
rest, and would bring two hundred francs. Why did you not take
them along with the plates?" As the soldiers release Valjean and
withdraw, Monseigneur Bienvenu draws close and speaks life-
changing words of grace: "Jean Valjean, my brother: you belong
no longer to evil, but to good. It is your soul that I am buying
for you. I withdraw it from dark thoughts and from the spirit of
perdition, and I give it to God!"

Later that night, after stumbling through the day in a stupor,
Valjean's eyes open to his sin.

> At the very moment when he exclaimed: "What a wretch I
> am!" he saw himself as he was, and was already so far sepa-
> rated from himself that it seemed to him that he was only a
> phantom, and that he had there before him, in flesh and bone

with his stick in his hand, his blouse on his back, his knapsack filled with stolen articles on his shoulders, with his stern and gloomy face, and his thoughts full of abominable projects, the hideous galley slave, Jean Valjean. . . .
He beheld himself then, so to speak, face to face. . . . Jean Valjean wept long. He shed hot tears, he wept bitterly. . . . He beheld his life, and it seemed to him horrible; his soul, and it seemed to him frightful. There was, however, a softened light upon that life and upon that soul. It seemed to him that he was looking upon Satan by the light of Paradise.[3]

In the presence of grace we can afford to open our eyes to our brokenness and honestly confront our sin. Sometimes we assume that places of grace begin with open and frank confession. Maybe we have it backward. Maybe open confession begins with the promise of grace. Or maybe they fit together such that we can no longer tell which comes first.

> Sometimes we assume that places of grace begin with open and frank confession. Maybe we have it backward. Maybe open confession begins with the promise of grace.

A colleague remembers the time she first experienced grace. She was a college student at the time, dating a young man she hoped she would marry. Their relationship was deepening, and she felt a need to tell him some things about herself, some things that were not pleasant. "When I started to talk to him that night, I couldn't find words. For fifteen minutes I could only cry. I felt so ashamed of what I was going to say. All that time he just held me, saying nothing, giving me time. In the end I was able to confess everything to him, and he embraced me with comfort. He accepted me despite the shameful things I told him." My friend married that young man, and now, more than thirty years later, she says, "I can tell that man anything. There is nothing my husband doesn't know about me." Hidden between the lines of her story is another truth: She can be honest with herself because she has a place of grace where she can be honest with another. What a winsome picture of grace. In places of grace such as this we can dare to tell the truth to ourselves and to the other.

After many years of providing psychotherapy and studying the scientific literature on its effectiveness, I am convinced that good therapy works because it is a place that emulates grace. It is a place of acceptance and mercy, a place where sin and the consequences of sin can be openly explored without the fear of judgment. This frees people to look honestly at themselves, to become more open in their other relationships, and to move forward into richer and deeper connections with those they love. Sadly, some therapists have lost the language of personal sin and focus only on how the client has been hurt by others. Others have overcompensated by focusing exclusively on personal sin and neglecting the ways clients have been harmed by others. In either case such therapy is rendered half-effective. A place of grace needs to be a place of open exploration and acceptance, where both sin and the consequences of sin can be named and grieved. In short, psychotherapy works because of its faint resemblance to the greatest story of all time.

Greg was released from his pastorate when his adulterous affair became known, and he hobbled into my office for some help pulling his life back together. Predictably, he was defensive at first, minimizing what he had done and the pain he had caused his family and congregation. Rather than confront his self-deception, I listened and cared for this broken man. Greg had never known mercy, so he could not afford to speak a language of sin. Paradoxically, he had preached many sermons about sin and grace, but these were theological concepts, ideas from books read in seminary rather than transforming life experiences. Raised in a family where he could never quite please his demanding parents, Greg married a good woman who had difficulty affirming him, and he entered a profession where perfection is the only tolerable standard. Greg had spent a lifetime running from his sin, never admitting his weakness because there were no arms of mercy to catch him if he fell.

My job was to catch him. As he began to feel safe—after several weeks of meeting together—his tears began to flow. His sin came into focus. Greg began to see the horrible truth of how he had betrayed his wife, children, and congregation. He shed tears of sorrow over his sin. He grieved his childhood, how he had longed for someone to express tender care for him regardless of his grades or athletic prowess. Greg spoke words of repentance and begged loved ones for forgiveness. This time his words were not from theology books but from his heart. He spoke and wept the language of sin, but only after he had a glimpse of grace.

The story of your life and mine—whether we know it or not— is about a place of grace more complete than we can imagine. God extends grace despite our unworthiness and our woundedness, embracing us as we speak the truth of our waywardness and offering eternal forgiveness. In this story God pursues us, dodging the barriers of our sinful choices, suffering when we suffer, smiling at our joys, longing for us to respond, patiently waiting for us to see a glimpse of divine love though we can only see it "as in a poor mirror" tarnished by the sinfulness of our world.[4] The New Testament states it succinctly: "God is love."[5]

➔ THE GREATEST STORY OF ALL

The human story began with exquisite beauty and goodness. No words can capture the perfection of God's creation, and even if pictures are worth a thousand words, no pictures could capture the brilliant colors and vivid depth of a garden teeming with life and joy and hope. Even if our imaginations could capture a thousand pictures, even then our imaginations fall far short of knowing the beauty of that place. We may think we know how birds sing in the springtime, but it's probably only a faint shadow of the way birds were made to sing—just a sound bite suffocated by the white noise. It is magnificent to be able to see the world with color vision, but maybe the green we see today is only a faint shadow of the rich, verdant green that God initially created. In the beginning was pure beauty. God spared no effort to create the perfect space for the beloved ones. God walked with them in the Garden. They longed to be with God, and God longed to be with them. Everything was as it should be. The depth of God's love was seen everywhere.

When sin shattered a perfect creation, everything changed. It's not just that we sin or that we are sinned against, it's that everything is different from the way God intended it to be, and all of these differences can be attributed to the consequences of sin. In his award-winning book, Cornelius Plantinga—now president of Calvin Seminary—reminds us our world is *Not the Way It's Supposed to Be.*[6] There are weeds in our gardens now, and in our personalities. Since the Fall, creation now groans with birth defects and disease and poverty. Our cars break down, our computers freeze in the midst of writing an important document, and we don't understand our friends, children, and spouses as well as they wish. Insects bite and swarm, viruses attack and mutate, vegetables rot. Humans create machines that harm the ozone layer. We get sunburned, have angina and congestive heart failure, become depressed and suicidal, crave all sorts of attachments, and develop addictions. Everything around us is broken. Things are not the way they are supposed to be.

My former colleague Tim Phillips used to make this point in his systematic theology classes by referring to weather patterns. "If you don't believe the world is fallen," he would say, "try living through a Chicago winter." Now this may take the point of a sinful world too far, but I use this example because Tim himself illustrates a world in which things are not right. In 2000, at the age of fifty, Tim lost a long struggle with cancer. At his memorial service one of our colleagues made the point that Tim would want us to know that this is not the way it is supposed to be. In contrast to a Pelagian view, in which decay and death are viewed as part of the original creation, most Christians stand in the Augustinian tradition, in which decay and death are viewed as the disastrous by-products of sin in our fallen world. Tim died—as our friends and family members do, and as all of us ultimately will—because the world isn't right. God, in divine sovereignty, allowed Tim to die, but I imagine God wept alongside all of Tim's friends and family. This is not right. This is not the way it is supposed to be. "Against its will, everything on earth was subjected to God's curse. All creation anticipates the day when it will join God's children in glorious freedom from death and decay. For we know that all creation has been groaning as in the pains of childbirth right up to the present time."[7]

Look around. Something is terribly wrong. This sin problem is bigger and more powerful than we know.

Abraham Kuyper, the nineteenth-century Dutch Reformed theologian, distinguished between what he called *normalists* and *abnormalists*. Normalists believe the current state of the world is basically normal. Though they acknowledge pain and suffering in the world, they see little point in pining for something better because there is nothing better. For example, because all plants and animals eventually die, death is viewed as normal.[8] The only sure source of knowledge, then, is found in studying the world as we currently experience it. Abnormalists believe that something is fundamentally wrong about the world, and it cries out for restoration, renewal, and redemption. Christians, at least those in the Augustinian tradition, are abnormalists. We believe that things are not right, that something went terribly wrong to spoil a perfect creation, that we are now living in a broken state, and that some-day all will be restored. Though every daffodil and lizard and human will eventually die, it does not mean that death is normal. Death is part of the curse of sin, reminding us how far all creation has fallen. Something is not right.

But however messed up our abnormal world may be, the story is not over yet. The Christian story is ultimately a comedy and not a tragedy; it ends as it began. Someday, there will be a new heaven and a new earth. Birds will really sing. Lions and lambs will tumble and play in grass that is truly green. Our bodies won't be riddled with wrinkles, muscle spasms, and cancer. There will be pure joy and beauty and goodness. And God, who longs to be with us, will walk with us in the Garden.

That may sound frightening or intimidating now—but it won't then. No ecstasy in this broken world will ever compare with our joy then, as we walk with God. We will be home. And it won't just be a story about a prodigal son or daughter who could never be good enough to earn God's favor. It will be a story about a loving God who delights in offering lavish, exuberant love. The depth of God's love will be seen everywhere.

→ ADMITTING SIN

In the context of this great story, surrounded by the love of God, we find enough safety to admit our sinfulness and the wounds of living in a sinful world. There is no risk in admitting how sinful and broken we are once we learn to rest in the comfort of God's love. We wrongly assume that a vocabulary of sin leads to self-hate, discouragement, or depression. On the contrary, once we see ourselves as sinners, we can stop trying to earn God's favor and learn to rest in God's arms. In the safety of God's love we can afford to look honestly at ourselves, experience contrition, and confess our wrongdoing. Augustine wrote in his *Confessions*, "I will now call to mind my past foulness and the carnal corruptions of my soul, not because I love them, but that I may love you, O my God."[9]

Seeing ourselves as sinners means we can stop trying to prove we are good enough. We are not. But we are loved. And God's love ushers in every good thing.

> We wrongly assume that a vocabulary of sin leads to self-hate, discouragement, or depression. On the contrary, once we see ourselves as sinners, we can stop trying to earn God's favor and learn to rest in God's arms.

This sort of heavenly love seeps down into our earthly relationships with one another. One friend hurts another. The offense stings, and the friendship suffers. This suffering may go on for a few minutes, several days, or many years until the offender crosses the desert and says, "I'm sorry. I was wrong. I know I hurt you." In the best friendships—the kind we all long for—the wounded one forgives and embraces the repentant sinner. Rarely is it this simple. Usually the offenses go both directions, and so confession and forgiveness must also. Sometimes one person sees no need to confess to the other, making forgiveness difficult and reconciliation impossible. Occasionally forgiveness seems too costly, and the offended one chooses to nurse bitterness. Sometimes the offense has been so costly that reconciliation is not wise. But in the best cases—those we celebrate in art and literature—confession is heartfelt, forgiveness profound, and the relationship restored. We all yearn for friendships such as this, for places of grace, where love can be known and shared.

The language of sin is not about feeling puny or demeaning ourselves. It is a language that cries out, along with all creation, for redemption. It is a language that celebrates goodness, that clings to the promise of true life in God and among God's people. With every human relationship, every place of grace, we see God's relational image at work. Whenever we find meaningful relationships with marriage partners, children, parents, friends, coworkers, and relatives, we are seeing a glimpse of God's love. There is a story to celebrate, and the language of sin calls us to the party.

→ PLEADING GUILTY

Some people stand outside the house, refusing to join the party—older brothers trying to compute who is better than whom, who deserves the harshest punishment—and refusing to make sense of this radical, backward notion of extending grace to sinners. Meanwhile the house is filled with dancing prodigals celebrating redemption, reveling in the grace of a loving Father.

> *There is a story to celebrate, and the language of sin calls us to the party.*

What keeps us standing outside in judgment? Fear, I think. If I show myself to be the prodigal I am, will someone be there to embrace me, or will I end up falling from grace, landing on a stone-cold slab of human disapproval? The risks are monumental and so very frightening. Can I even bear to tell myself the truth, or shall I just retreat again into the safety of denial? Pleading guilty requires enormous courage. It begs for the promise of grace.

Jeff's life was punctured with truth one rainy Seattle afternoon as police confronted him about sexually abusing two of his high school students. Eleven years later he agreed to tell his story for this book, so Jeff and I sat in our offices, connected by twenty-five hundred miles of telephone wire, both fighting back tears as we discussed the events that followed that dismal March day. Today he is restored because he found the courage to plead guilty.

There were those who felt he could have won his case in court. Both girls were eighteen years old or older, the sexual touching appeared to be consensual, and his attorney assured him that he had never lost a case such as this. Though Jeff felt morally guilty and utterly broken by the personal failure in his life, he did not see how he was legally guilty of sexual abuse. So with the advice of his attorney he pleaded "not guilty" and for a season entered into the labyrinth of legalese, court dates, and self-protection.

It did not last. Five months into the legal maneuvering Jeff had a moment of awakening while reading a book about sexual sin. He recognized how he had abused his power, taking advantage of two young women who were vulnerable and confused in his presence. The weight of his sin and the voice of God descended on him in a flash of truth. Jeff recalled, "If I have ever heard an audible voice from God, a voice screaming out in my soul, this was the time. I had been struggling to understand my guilt, and God was gracious enough to put it in print."

He sat motionless in his kitchen, face flushed, heart pounding, knowing what he had to do. He stood, walked to the family room, and told his wife he needed to change his plea. With her support, and despite the protests and warning of his attorney, he pleaded "no contest" and was sentenced with various consequences, including time in jail. He described great peace in his decision: "Once I knew I was doing the right thing—and it was refreshing to know I was doing the right thing—I realized the consequences are going to last for only so long. It's the illicit things that are so awful."

A year before Jeff was arrested in Washington, Carl—a youth pastor—was detained in Arizona for similar charges. Three high school girls accused him of sexual abuse, charges were filed, and he was brought in for questioning. Like Jeff, Carl found a good attorney, pleaded "not guilty," and entered months of discovery and legal proceedings. Unlike Jeff, Carl was never able to admit his sin. Even after investigators uncovered Carl's criminal record in another state, where he was convicted for a similar offense, he insisted he was just hugging the girls, simply displaying encouragement and affection when they seemed down. The court decided otherwise, and Carl spent several months in jail, still protesting his conviction and proclaiming his innocence.

Perhaps Jeff was willing to admit his guilt because he had a loving community that would catch him. Or maybe it is the other way around: he found love and support in others because he was willing to speak the language of sin. For whatever reason, whether it was lack of supportive community, lack of insight, or lack of courage, Carl could not speak the language of sin. Today Jeff is reunited with family, delighted with his two sons, happy in his marriage, and restored to meaningful work. Carl lives alone in a Yuma trailer court, estranged from family and friends, still declaring his innocence.

I fear I paint this picture too simply. Pleading guilty is no easy task. Jeff's world collapsed with his arrest. Three pillars crashed in around him. The first crash was an awareness of his moral failure. Years of living a duplicitous life, his conscience, gradually calloused by secret sins, now stared him in the face. As his transgressions accumulated, so did fear and secrecy. Speaking about his sin was terrifying. Yet he knew the local media were about to do it for him. His wife was the first person he went to after leaving the police station, anticipating she would ask him to leave. "She chose to love and forgive me. It was unbelievable." Such forgiveness is never easy. Jeff and Carolyn found a good marital therapist. Jeff also received individual therapy and became part of a twelve-step group. It must have taken Carolyn years to fully forgive, and yet she stayed by his side, loving and supporting him. Jeff wonders how Carolyn could choose "to stand in the fire with the one who embarrassed and betrayed her." And his close friends stood by him too, despite their shock. Jeff fell into the arms of a loving partner and compassionate friends.

The second crash was the loss of reputation. Part of a small community, Jeff could no longer go to the grocery store, a Little League game, a school program, church, or even mow his lawn or drive down the street without experiencing overwhelming feelings of shame. After confessing to his wife, he next went to his pastor to speak of his sin. He wanted to pack up and leave, to run as far as possible from this church where he worshiped and served. With kindness and beautiful grace his pastor replied, "You ought to just stay here and let us love you." The next Sunday, though his attorney had advised him not to speak to anyone about his wrongdoing, he confessed his sin in nonspecific ways to the congregation and asked their forgiveness. Instead of booing or throwing hymnals, they surrounded him—literally surrounded him, arms outstretched—with love and support. Jeff recalls, "I just went back to my seat and was sobbing, and they all just came and loved me. And that was so amazing. And it gave me strength to keep pursuing the truth." Jeff fell into the arms of a loving community—God's love embodied in people willing to extend forgiveness.

The third crash was his job loss. Highly successful as a teacher, Jeff immediately resigned and soon lost his teaching certificate. A part-time minister at his church, he stepped down from that position also. He worked odd jobs to make ends meet, but even here he saw God's redemptive hand. Working in a manual labor position gave him the opportunity to reflect on his needy state and to allow God to build important character qualities in his life. Many years later, when a full-time job opened at the same church, he was restored to a position of ministry. When Jeff talks about his new ministry position, his voice quivers with gratitude. He never dreamed of being restored to ministry, yet God saw fit to allow him to serve the same congregation that cared so dearly for him a decade earlier. Jeff fell into the arms of a loving God.

Jeff's world caved in around him—his moral failure suffocating him, his reputation ruined, and his job gone. But in each case he fell into arms of grace, and he has been restored. Carl tried frantically to hold his world together: denying his moral failure, clinging to his reputation, and insisting it was unfair for the church to fire him. One claimed the language of sin; the other avoided it. One fell into arms of grace; the other refused to fall anywhere. One lives in community, surrounded by love and hope, the other lives alone, surrounded by denial and loss.

After dragging Jeff back through his story during our telephone conversation, I expressed appreciation and told him I was sorry to make him relive difficult memories. His response surprised me: "It is hard to bring it up again, but in a way I don't ever want to forget it. I don't want to forget the power"—his voice choked with emotion—"the power and the grace and the forgiveness of God. I was so afraid that I would be abandoned and cast off. Fear is what kept me hidden; that's what gave sin tremendous power in my life. Exactly that. I was terribly afraid. But that great fear of abandonment and rejection was just a lie. I don't ever want to forget that."

→ GOOD NEWS, BAD NEWS

There is both good news and bad news imbedded in the truth that we are all sinners. The metaphysical reality of sin is terrible—as bad as it gets. Being sinners means we are wounded, we wound others, and we live in a global community where various wounds confound and magnify small problems until they become huge problems. Sin keeps us far from God, and far from one another. Sin is truly terrible.

But the language of sin—acknowledging this terrible thing that happened to all creation—is a good thing. Pleading guilty, admitting our fallen, broken state opens the possibility of repentance and allows us to clean out wounds. James Bryan Smith, an author and spiritual leader, writes, "Now we can stop lying to ourselves. We are saved from our own self-deception the moment we say with the tax collector, 'God be merciful to me, *a sinner*' (Luke 18:13). We no longer need to apply cosmetics to make ourselves more acceptable to God. We have been accepted by God, and therefore, we can accept ourselves."[10]

Sinners experience contrition, they repent, they are forgiven, embraced, and reconciled. Grace is possible when we acknowledge our sin, and we can acknowledge our sin when we see the promise of grace. In one of his prayers Nouwen reflects: "An avoidance of a confrontation with my real sinfulness means also an avoidance of a confrontation with your mercy. As long as I have not experienced your mercy I know that I am still running away from my real sin."[11]

Part of our brokenness is that we turn this all upside down. We are products of an era that tells us it's a bad thing to think of ourselves as sinners. We think the language of sin leads to self-hatred, judgment, and criticism. So we exchange a vocabulary that brings the possibility of deep healing for cheap alternatives that offer few solutions. We trade the deepest longing of our souls— to love and be loved by another—for a therapeutic language of self-love. We posture ourselves, trying to decide whom we should blame, who has the codependency problem, who is addicted to what, whose boundaries are sloppy, which parent is to blame, and who most desperately needs therapy. These other languages can sometimes be useful, but they do not carry the hope for healing found in the language of sin and grace.

The story of sin is the story of God's grace.

PART TWO

THE
DAMAGE
REPORT

FIVE

{ *Disordered Passions* }

Almost every major newspaper could be subtitled *The Daily Damage Report.* On one page we read of the devastating effects of a coastal hurricane, the next page tallies the lives lost in the latest military skirmish, and the next describes how many layoffs are being caused by a sputtering economic engine. Between occasional human interest stories we see page after page of damage. Murders, accidents, health epidemics, manufacturer recalls, fires, and corporate corruption all remind us things are not right.

As we see the story of sin, we begin to see what a mess we're in. The damage report is extensive. We see it all around us. Nations battle over ideological and political differences. Terrorists blow themselves up so they can kill a few civilians they hate.

U.S. citizens enjoy an average per capita income of $34,000 while people in Ethiopia earn the equivalent of $100.[1] One-fifth of the earth's population uses 86 percent of its resources.[2] Some of us build home theaters or backyard swimming pools while others stand in food lines or watch their children die of starvation. Basic health care is not available to some people, while others spend their health-care dollars for things such as liposuction. Workers all over the globe are exposed to hazardous conditions in the name of profit. Mercury, lead, and cadmium from our throwaway electronics become tomorrow's toxic waste. Jobs in urban centers wane as corporations follow the white flight to the suburbs. Racism lives on.

So does cancer. AIDS ravages the world, especially in Africa and Asia. Pollution, urban poverty, and crime threaten the great cities of the world. The world's prisons are full.

Sexual harassment plagues the workplace and sneaks in the back door of our houses of worship. Illegal drugs make a few wrongfully wealthy while gripping many more in the claws of addiction and desperation. Divorce and premature death rip families apart. Families struggle with hidden problems of abuse and violence while single parents deal with the stress of "doing it all." Promiscuity persists as sexually transmitted diseases proliferate. Internet pornography sneaks its way into good homes, tearing apart husbands and wives, parents and children.

If this catalog of sin is overwhelming, it is meant to be. Sin ricochets around our homes and communities, our churches and our nations, and everyone is wounded as a result.[3] Things are a mess.

We could look at the damage report from many different perspectives, and each would be valuable. Political scientists might look at ideological tensions and international relations. Sociologists consider problems of injustice and oppression. Historical theologians examine the Seven Deadly Sins. Environmental biochemists look at problems of toxic waste. As a psychologist, my tendency is to look at individuals and families. What I offer in the next three chapters is only a small subset of the damage report as seen through the eyes of a Christian psychologist.

➔ THE HEART OF THE MATTER

When speaking of sin, it is quite natural to look at the "big" sins of others. We may think of sinners as those other people who embezzle, murder, oppress, and abuse. This externalizes sin, making it someone else's problem. But if we trace back the roots of the "big" sins, we find they begin in a place familiar to each of us: in the dark shadows of the human heart. Jesus taught, "From the heart come evil thoughts, murder, adultery, all other sexual immorality, theft, lying, and slander. These are what defile you."[4]

Jesus was not a cardiologist; he was not referring to throbbing atria or pulmonary arteries. The heart has always been a metaphor for the affections of the inner life. Jesus knew the human heart well. He knew it is a place where purity, love, faith, and hope can be found.[5] Jesus also knew that the heart is dangerous, that it can be hard, and that it can spawn greed and adultery.[6] Our hearts are complex, made to mirror God's image, and yet that mirror is marred with sin.

The human heart pulses with paradox. One moment my heart soars in the beauty of corporate worship, and in the next moment I am complaining that the worship songs were pitched too high or that the pastor spoke a few minutes too long. My heart connects with my lifelong partner as we lie in bed for a morning chat and exchange tender words, but then an hour later I become grumpy, demanding, and difficult to please. My heart finds its most profound repose in prayer, in communion with God, yet my prayer is bombarded with intrusive thoughts of ambition and self-absorption. My heart allows me to set aside my own interests and provide a kindness to another, and then I smugly elevate myself by assuming that I am a better person than the one I am helping. With

> The human heart pulses with paradox.

my heart I experience peaceful contentment as I witness the simple goodness of a virgin forest or a snow-capped mountain, and then I climb back into a fossil-fuel-guzzling 767 to fly back home.

Our hearts are complex, easily deceived, and enormously beautiful. Our hearts draw us to the heights of humanity, to places of joy, faith, goodness, hope, compassion, and mercy. When our hearts are aligned well, the great commandments become palpable: love God with singular devotion and love our neighbor as we love ourselves.[7] We love with our hearts, and love is the source of all good things.

We hear a great deal about the spiritual disciplines these days. Highly acclaimed books such as Richard Foster's *The Celebration of Discipline* and Dallas Willard's *The Spirit of the Disciplines* remind today's Christians of what believers in previous centuries knew well: our hearts need regular spiritual practices.[8] The various disciplines—prayer, meditation, fasting, solitude, confession, silence, worship, and others—allow us to experience God's grace and to help align the passions of our hearts. These disciplines are risky, though, because it is easy to begin feeling smug or arrogant in our spiritual practices. When the disciplines become an end in themselves, we are inclined to rank ourselves according to spiritual sophistication. Sixteen centuries ago church leader John Cassian noted that the purpose of the disciplines is to order our passions—to align our hearts—and that the purpose of ordered passions is to love. Simply put, the disciplines train us to follow the Great Commandment of loving God and others.

In our sinful state, our passions are disordered. We fail to love well because our hearts are misaligned. Loving God becomes religious rhetoric, and loving another as oneself becomes an excuse for building self-esteem. We turn it upside down, as Alvin Plantinga notes: "Instead of loving God above all and my neighbor as myself, I am inclined to love myself above all and, indeed, to hate God and my neighbor. Much of this hatred and hostility springs from *pride*, that aboriginal sin, and from consequent attempts at self-aggrandizement."[9]

> *We fail to love well because our hearts are misaligned.*

The damage report of sin begins with the condition of the human heart.

➤ PRIDE AND THE PRODIGAL

The top line of the damage report, first on the list, is pride. For centuries pride has been considered chief among the deadly sins—the sin from which other evils emerge.[10] Commenting on pride, C. S. Lewis writes:

> According to Christian teachers, the essential vice, the utmost evil, is Pride. Unchastity, anger, greed, drunkenness, and all that, are mere fleabites in comparison: it was through Pride that the devil became the devil: Pride leads to every other vice: it is the complete anti-God state of mind.
>
> Does this seem to you to be exaggerated? If so, think it over. I pointed out a moment ago that the more pride one had, the more one disliked pride in others. In fact, if you want to find out how proud you are the easiest way is to ask yourself, "How much do I dislike it when other people snub me, or refuse to take any notice of me, or shove their oar in, or patronize me, or show off?" The point is that each person's pride is in competition with every one else's pride. It is because I want to be the big noise at the party that I am so annoyed at someone else being the big noise.[11]

The power of the Prodigal Son parable is that we see ourselves when we look closely. We may not see ourselves in the prodigal by looking at his extreme choices—sleeping with prostitutes and squandering his money on wild parties—but if we look closer and see that the root of his problem was pride, we see ourselves. His capacity to love had been turned upside down, and he loved self above all. He marched off with disordered passions, in selfish independence, thinking the rules did not apply to him, that he would be smart enough or strong enough to avoid trouble. His sinful pride led him to a faraway land of tragedy. How often do we follow our pride to places of self-absorption and arrogant independence?

If it is difficult to see ourselves in the prodigal, Jesus gave us another prideful character to consider. In the biblical story (though not in Rembrandt's painting) the older brother refuses to enter the house and begrudges the party given the younger son. He makes a compelling case: "All these years I've worked hard for you and never once refused to do a single thing you told me to. And in all that time you never gave me even one young goat for a feast with my friends. Yet when this son of yours comes back after squandering your money on prostitutes, you celebrate by killing the finest calf we have."[12]

I suspect that as Jesus told the parable to the Pharisees, they nodded to each other, affirming the older brother's thinking. In Nouwen's book *The Return of the Prodigal Son,* he discusses how he immediately identified with the prodigal and then later—with the help of a friend—began seeing himself more in the older brother. Nouwen acknowledges a covert form of pride, one that looks smugly on those caught in the grip of overt sin while quietly believing that we deserve more because we have not fallen to the same depth. It's not "I'm a mess, you're a mess," but "I'm OK, you're a mess." Or perhaps it is, "You're a mess, and I used to be a mess." This subtle form of pride neglects the pervasive grasp that sin has on every life.

Not surprisingly then, one of the clearest conclusions from social science research is that we are proud. We think we are better than we really are, we see our faults in faint black and white rather than in vivid color, and we assume the worst in others while assuming the best in ourselves. Because of pride we follow our hearts to faraway places where disaster awaits.

→ INFLATED SELF-ASSESSMENTS

The essence of pride is that we place ourselves above others. Like
Yogi Bear—who claimed to be "smarter than the average bear"—
most of us see ourselves as smarter than we really are. We also
claim to be better leaders, better workers, better parents and
spouses, better friends, and better money managers. Who wants
to be average? So we convince ourselves we are above average.

By definition most people are average on most traits. On almost
any trait, such as intelligence or anxiety or affability, most people
cluster around the middle of a
bell-shaped distribution. In fact,
68 percent of the population falls
within the average range. With
intelligence tests, for example, 68
percent of the population scores
between 85 and 115. An addi-
tional 16 percent is above average, and 16 percent is below average.

> *The essence of pride is
> that we place ourselves
> above others.*

If we perceived ourselves accurately, then when asked how intelligent we are, 68 percent of us would put ourselves somewhere in
the average range, 16 percent above average, 16 percent below
average, and so on. But that is not what happens when people are
asked how intelligent they are. Most people—almost everyone—
will say they are at least average. Many more than 16 percent will
say they are above average. And this is not only true for intelligence
but also for any positive trait measured. The graphic on page 70
illustrates how we see ourselves more favorably than we really are.

Stephen Moroney, a Malone College professor of philosophy
and theology with training and expertise in social psychology,
offers some fascinating examples of inflated self-assessments.[13]
When the Educational Testing Service asked nearly one million
high school students how well they got along with their peers, all
of them rated themselves as average or above; of those, 60 percent

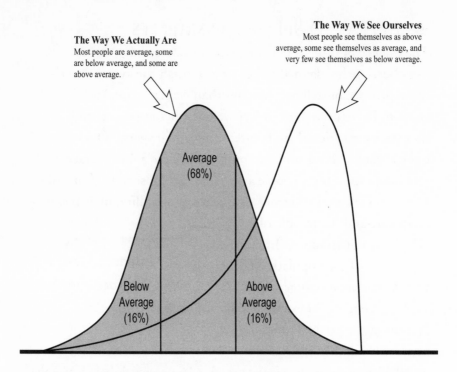

The Way We Actually Are
Most people are average, some
are below average, and some are
above average.

The Way We See Ourselves
Most people see themselves as above
average, some see themselves as average, and
very few see themselves as below average.

Average
(68%)

Below
Average
(16%)

Above
Average
(16%)

believed themselves to be in the top 10 percent, and 25 percent
believed themselves to be in the top 1 percent.

What about college professors? Certainly these educated elite
would have accurate perceptions of their abilities, right? Nope.
When college professors were asked to rate the quality of their
teaching, they were not any more realistic than the high school
students. Two percent reported they were below average, 10
percent saw themselves as average, 63 percent described themselves
as above average, and 25 percent said they were truly exceptional.
This, of course, is statistically impossible.

None of us wants to be average or below, so we simply fix
the problem by perceiving ourselves to be above average. This
elevates our view of ourselves above what it ought to be and
relegates others to a lower position.

Our prideful tendency toward self-serving comparison has

implications for everyday life. In the midst of an argument with a loved one, we rarely conclude, "Her opinion is better reasoned than mine." Instead, our pride leads us to say, "I can't believe how stupid she is being. Why can't she see this the right way?" We assume our opinions and beliefs to be better than those of others. If I recall a memory differently from how someone else recalls it, I assume my recollection is correct and the other person is confused. Augustine confessed that he "disdained to be a little one. Swollen with pride, I looked on myself as a great one."[14]

This is part of our brokenness, part of the damage report. Our passions are disordered, and our ability to love is skewed. As a result, we think of ourselves more highly than we ought.

In the New Testament the apostle Paul wrote, "As God's messenger, I give each of you this warning: Be honest in your estimate of yourselves, measuring your value by how much faith God has given you."[15] Most of us seem to have excessive faith in ourselves and not enough faith in the opinions of others. The prodigal certainly did when he took his money against all cultural wisdom and ran off to a faraway land. The older brother did when he perceived his punitive reaction to be more fitting than his father's grace.

> *Our passions are disordered, and our ability to love is skewed. As a result we think of ourselves more highly than we ought.*

➔ HOLIER THAN SO-AND-SO

Not only do we perceive ourselves as more capable than we really are, we also perceive ourselves to be more upright and moral than most others. One polling expert put it this way: "It's the great contradiction: the average person believes he is a better person than the average person."[16] Sixteen centuries earlier Augustine bemoaned: "[My] sin was all the more incurable because I did not judge myself to be a sinner."[17]

People's overestimation of themselves is a robust finding in social science. People think they are better than others—more ethical, considerate, industrious, cooperative, fair, and loyal. People think they obey the Ten Commandments more consistently than others. We do this not so much because we underestimate others but because we overestimate ourselves. Our tendency is to see others as the sinners they are and to see ourselves as the perfected saints we are not.

Long before social scientists discovered our tendency to think too highly of our spiritual virtues, religious and devotional writers were saying the same thing. Back in the eighteenth century the great American theologian Jonathan Edwards warned about our prideful tendencies: "It can be recognized when one compares himself to others when he thinks he is an eminent saint in comparison. . . . 'I am holier than you' (Isaiah 65:5). In taking the high place, they are doing what Christ condemns (Luke 14:7). They are confident that they are guides to the blind, but they are the blind in actuality (Romans 2:19, 20). But he whose heart is subject to Christian humility has a very different attitude. For humility, or true lowliness of mind, causes people to think others better than themselves (Philippians 2:3)."[18]

> *Our tendency is to see others as the sinners they are and to see ourselves as the perfected saints we are not.*

I am reminded of the older brother in Rembrandt's painting. He stands in judgment, his face expressing something like the sentiment voiced by the religious leader praying in the temple: "I thank you, God, that I am not a sinner like everyone else."[19] If we strain to see it, we glimpse this older brother in ourselves. Nouwen writes: "It is hard for me to concede that this bitter, resentful, angry man might be closer to me in a spiritual way than the lustful younger brother. Yet the more I think about the elder son, the more I recognize myself in him."[20]

If you are a churchgoer, do you ever get the sense that we come together as a fellowship of older brothers, thanking God that we are not like others, all the while failing to see the bitterness and resentment in our own souls? How easy it is to stand in judgment. How difficult it is to see ourselves in all our brokenness and pride. Jonathan Edwards writes: "Many religious people tend to hide and cover up the corruption of their own hearts so that they do not see themselves as they are before God."[21] How easy it is to be the older brother.

I wonder sometimes what our church experience would look like if we were a fellowship of prodigals, a community of ragamuffins?[22] What would it look like to cling only to God's mercy and to let go of our reputations, our need for respect, and our bitterness for how others have behaved? What if we were more like the steward in Rembrandt's painting, leaning in to glimpse God's mercy, or like the temple tax collector who does not even dare to raise his eyes to heaven but beats his chest and cries out, "O God, be merciful to me, for I am a sinner"?[23]

Even as I write this, I think to myself how much better church might be if *other* people saw themselves more like the prodigal, the steward, or the tax collector. *Other* people. My mind goes wild: "Yes, so-and-so needs to be more like a prodigal and less like an older brother," and in thinking this, I have again become the older brother: critical, judgmental, holier than so-and-so. No wonder it's so hard to change the church—it's so hard to change myself, and the church is made up of people like me.

→ EXPLAINING AWAY OUR FAILURES

The damage report continues, as the evidence of human pride is monumental and unarguable. We have already considered how we

73

estimate ourselves to be more capable and more moral than we really are. We also reveal a pride problem in how we perceive our own successes and failures as well as those of others.

When something bad happens, we tend to explain it by saying it is someone else's fault. It wasn't a fair test, the person next to me was making noise, the professor teaches poorly, and so on. Five-year-old Johnny runs into his parents' room and explains how he was counting sheep when one of them wet the bed. Something bad happens, blame the sheep. So how do we explain good outcomes? Scores of research studies demonstrate that we tend to take personal credit when good things happen (I deserve it, I am a hard worker, I am smart, and so on).

Think about the implications. When something bad happens, we blame others. When something good happens, we take credit for it. A person wins the chess game because he's smart; he loses because the other player was distracting him by humming. She gets hired because she is talented; she is not hired because another applicant is willing to compromise ethics to get ahead. If people like the sermon, it's because the preacher is a good speaker; if people fall asleep, it's because they are obstinate. Our pride allows us to recast the story so that we look acceptable regardless of the outcome.

> When something bad happens to us, we blame others; but when something bad happens to others, we tend to explain it as being their own fault.

It gets even more complicated when looking at bad events that happen to others. When something bad happens to us, we blame others; but when something bad happens to others, we tend to explain it as being their own fault. If something bad happens to you, it's your fault. If something bad happens to me, it's still your fault. When I fail the exam, it's because it was a bad test. However, when you fail, it's because you did not study enough. When I get a speeding ticket, it's because the police officer needed to fill a quota at the end of the month. But when you get a speeding ticket, it's because you drive too fast. We blame others for their failures, and we blame them for ours too.

These attribution errors are not deliberate acts of sin; in fact, we are probably not even aware of them. When something bad happens, I don't go to the nearest Starbucks to sit and figure out whom to blame. My blaming someone else is an automatic reaction that occurs beneath conscious awareness, reflecting the disordered passions of my heart. It is part of the damage report.

Pause for a moment to consider the closest relationships in your life. Are some frayed by wounds of the past? Perhaps an insulating layer of defensiveness has built up over the years to a point where closeness seems cumbersome or impossible. Maybe you are disappointed in love. Sin exacts a toll where it costs the most—in our close connections with one another. Even if these frayed relationships haven't been jolted with the "big sins" of betrayal, they are still tainted by the daily sin of pride. We see ourselves more highly than we ought, and those we care about most have the same problem. We see others more negatively than we ought, and they look at us through the same negative filter. Over time it wears us down. We feel tired, burned out, fatigued by the work of closeness. And it's because we are sinners who live with other sinners, each of us beset with pride and disordered passions.

→ SELF-JUSTIFICATION

Another evidence of the damage report is our tendency to justify our behavior. We typically assume that we form well-reasoned opinions, and then we behave according to those opinions. For example, we decide what political candidate is most consistent with our political views, and then we vote accordingly. We take positions on controversial issues, and then we live in a way consistent with those positions. The assumption is that opinions come first and behavior follows.

Unfortunately, many decades of social science research demonstrate a more complex relationship between opinions and behaviors. More often than not, we first observe our behaviors and then craft our opinions to be consistent with those behaviors. In other words, we justify what we have already done by changing our beliefs.

I used to think I was a pacifist until a therapy client threatened my family. Then I found my grandfather's antique gun in the attic and hid it under my bed while I tried to sleep. Fortunately, I did not have to use the gun, but my behavior was different from my beliefs. Rather than conforming my behavior to my beliefs, I responded by changing my beliefs. I no longer call myself a pacifist.

It's no surprise that political candidates ask to have their campaign signs placed in people's yards—the candidates have been advised about the research findings. When people agree to have the signs placed in the yard, it changes their opinion about the candidate for the better. Politicians know that if they can get that sign in your yard, you are almost certain to vote for them, even if you would not have voted for them before agreeing to have the sign placed. We shift our opinions to be consistent with our behaviors.

It is uncommon for someone to make an expensive purchase and then regret it—not because expensive purchases are always wise, but because of self-justification. Someone may spend an excessive amount of money on a new luxury car, and if you ask a few days later, this person will invariably be pleased with the car: "The ride is smooth and quiet, it gets good mileage, and the warranty is excellent." Even if the price was well over the market value for the car, the purchaser will believe it was a good purchase because it would create too much inner conflict to admit otherwise.

Self-justification is a huge obstacle to acknowledging our sin. In our broken state we are masters at shifting our attitudes to match our behaviors. So we experience lust or envy, feel some immediate dissonance, and then decide that it really must not be that bad. Or we cheat on our taxes and then reason that it really isn't that bad because lots of other people cheat too. The human capacity to justify almost anything is frightening.

The "big" sins we might expect to be at the forefront of the damage report are all derived from that abhorrent condition that reflects the disordered passions of our hearts: pride. We compare ourselves in an unrealistically favorable light with others. We attribute good outcomes to ourselves and bad outcomes to others. When others have misfortune, we blame them. And we justify our behavior by changing our opinions after we act. We love ourselves more than we love others. The damage report looks serious.

→ AN ABSURD CONTRAST

Karl Barth, the twentieth-century Swiss theologian, demonstrates the absurdity of our pride by contrasting it with the humility of Jesus. Christians hold Jesus to be divine and eternal. The New Testament author John writes of Jesus: "In the beginning the Word already existed. He was with God, and he was God. He was in the beginning with God. He created everything there is. Nothing exists that he didn't make. Life itself was in him, and this life gives light to everyone."[24]

And yet Jesus, who is God, humbled himself. John goes on: "So the Word became human and lived here on earth among us. He was full of unfailing love and faithfulness."[25] What amazing humility! The God of the universe, the Creator of everything, becomes a child with flesh and blood in order to bridge the gap between God and humanity. Whenever I become cynical about the commercialism and materialism of Christmas, I retreat into Christian doctrine and remember the truth of the Incarnation: God became human. The eternal, all-powerful One gave it all up to become the small child lying in the filthy place where cows eat hay. That's how much God loves us.

Given the humility of Christ, it makes sense that we who follow Christ would also make every effort to be humble. The apostle Paul advises Christians in New Testament times to follow the example of Jesus: "Your attitude should be the same that Christ Jesus had. Though he was God, he did not demand and cling to his rights as God. He made himself nothing; he took the humble position of a slave and appeared in human form. And in human form he obediently humbled himself even further by dying a criminal's death on a cross."[26]

Here, of course, is where Barth recognizes an absurd contrast. Our pride—our tendency to perceive ourselves as better than we are, our inflated self-assessments—demonstrates how much we want to be like God. Meanwhile, God—the eternal and majestic Creator filled with all power, knowledge, and goodness—empties himself in the form of Jesus, even to the point of a violent and horrific death for trumped-up charges. In Augustine's words: "God is already humble though man is still proud."[27] It is absurd.

→ IS THERE HOPE?

If we are so prone to pride, so capable of self-deception, then where can we find hope for our broken souls? Finding hope calls us to reflect on the bigger story of our lives. Beneath the armor of our pride we live as vulnerable men and women longing to be loved and known. If the world were completely safe, then it would be easy to take off our armor and come together in caring community. But the world isn't safe, and it has not been for a very long time, so we live with armor. When we dare to bare ourselves, sometimes we find love and acceptance, but sometimes we find abuse and ridicule. So we make a calculated choice, perhaps unconsciously, to protect ourselves by hiding behind pride.

Beneath the armor of our pride we live as vulnerable men and women longing to be loved and known.

If our deepest longing in life is

to be someone important—to make a mark, to be the perfect parent, the top of the class, or the best employee—then we better keep the armor on. But what if all those goals are merely the glimmer of the armor, the distractions of disordered passions? What if the deeper yearning of the human soul is to love and be loved? Then our hope is found in cautiously shedding our armor in the safety of caring relationships, acknowledging that we are vulnerable and needy, and clinging to the possibility of love.

Why does sin matter? Because the language of sin is the way we shed the armor of prideful self-defense. In our contemporary preoccupation with self-esteem and personal accomplishment we have become adept at polishing the steel, but the inner self still longs for love more than self-love, for grace more than impression management, for authenticity more than admiration. All around us we see a renewed fascination with spirituality as people sift through the shrapnel of the Me Generation and reclaim the longing of the human soul.

Blaise Pascal, the seventeenth-century mathematician and philosopher, wrote: "Man is nothing but a subject full of natural error that cannot be eradicated except through grace."[28] Pascal implies two possibilities. Either we can spend our time denying our natural error, or we can set aside the armor and cry out for grace. Our hope is in grace, and reclaiming the language of sin gives us access to grace. When we spend all our efforts trying to convince ourselves and others that we are better than we really are, we only end up spinning a web of self-deception. But if we accept the truth and recognize how natural error pervades every

> *The inner self still longs for love more than self-love, for grace more than impression management, for authenticity more than admiration.*

part of our existence, then we invite grace into our relationships with one another and with God.

Who are the people you like most? Are they the people who deny their faults or those willing to admit their flaws? Most of us are drawn to the second group, to other prodigals and stewards who know they are imperfect. These are the folks who invite grace. If the home or the church is to be a place of grace and hope, it must also be a place where we see ourselves as "full of natural error" so that we embark on the path of grace. What a beautiful discipline it is to strain to find value in others' perspectives and to strain to find fault in our own.

Jonathan Edwards sees this necessity: "But the more eminent that saints are, the more they will have the light of heaven in their souls. Thus they will appear to themselves to be the more debased and sinful. They can only cover themselves with the righteousness of Christ, and allow their own deficiencies to be swallowed up and hid in the beams of His abundant glory and love."[29]

> If the home or the church is to be a place of grace and hope, it must also be a place where we see ourselves as "full of natural error" so that we embark on the path of grace.

Our great hope is found in looking ourselves straight in the eye, acknowledging our sinful pride. Few have done this better—or worse—than John Newton.

✦ WAS BLIND, BUT NOW I SEE (DIMLY)

Newton, author of one of the greatest hymns of all time, lived and told a story of sin and grace. *Amazing grace—how sweet the sound.*[30] I have often heard Christians speak of his powerful story: how Newton was once a slave trader who was gripped by God's love in the midst of a tumultuous storm on the high seas. *That saved a wretch like me.* So in preparing this book, I walked from my office across the Wheaton College campus to Buswell Memorial Library, weaved my way through the Dewey decimal maze to a fifty-three-year-old biography of Newton published by Bernard Martin thirteen years before Martin Luther King Jr. articulated his dream of freedom for all people. I drove home, plopped down on the living room sofa, and began reading about a life of amazing grace.

It was not what I expected.

Here is the way I wanted the story to go: Newton grows up in a culture in which slavery is commonplace and ends up lured by avarice into the slave-trading business. But then, during that awful storm in March of 1748, he sees the wretchedness of his greed and is sickened by his crimes against humanity. *I once was lost but now am found.* From that moment forward Newton turns against slavery, devotes himself to God, and becomes a tireless crusader against the horrendous social evil of slavery. His disordered passions suddenly become ordered. *Was blind but now I see.*

Despite my best wishes, this was not Newton's story.

It is true that Newton had some sort of awakening from a shockingly profane and blasphemous existence as he guided *The Greyhound*—a ship that carried gold, ivory, and beeswax rather than slaves—through mountainous ocean swells. Before Newton's devout mother died, when he was six, she had instilled in him some knowledge of God, and in these hours of almost certain death Newton returned to the faith of his youth. His blind eyes may have been opened on that dismal March night, but not wide enough to see the full extent of his sin and his culture's evil. The ship drifted for several weeks before finding the coast of northern Ireland. Newton stayed in Londonderry for six weeks as the ship was being repaired, attending prayer services, studying the Christian faith, and renouncing his former way of life. He later reflected: "I was no longer an infidel; I heartily renounced my former profaneness; I had taken up some right notions, was seriously disposed, and sincerely touched with a sense of the undeserving mercy I had received in being brought safely through so many dangers. I was sorry for my past misspent life, and purposed an immediate reformation. . . . yet still I was greatly deficient in many respects. . . . I was little aware of the innate evils of my heart."[31]

Indeed. Upon Newton's return to Liverpool he promptly signed on as mate of *The Brownlow,* a ship that sailed to Africa, where Newton relapsed into a life of sexual sin despite his commitment to Mary Catlett, his wife to be. Newton found himself "in a course of evil, of which, a few months before I could not have supposed myself any longer capable."[32] He later described himself as a dog returning to his vomit. These were obvious sins to Newton, arousing guilt and a desire to live better. But far more alarming was the abhorrent sin and disordered passions he could not see because his culture blinded him from the truth.

The Brownlow docked in the Sierra Leone River as Newton traveled from village to village buying slaves and returning them as cargo to the ship. He then sailed across the Atlantic, studying a Latin Bible in his quarters as two hundred slaves lay in the hull, shackled two by two, squeezed into shelves like secondhand books. As many as a third died during the long voyage across the ocean, and many more suffered serious illnesses. When the ship arrived in Charleston, South Carolina, Newton delivered the slaves into a life of toil and oppression while he sat in church services and took leisurely strolls through fields and woods outside Charleston.

Our eyes open slowly. Blinded by pride, we see through the culture of self-interest. We so naturally elevate our selves, families, communities above others and uncritically accept the social evils we perpetuate. Newton had no concept of slavery's being wrong—few Christians of his day did. Sometimes I wonder how blind I am, each of us are, to the cultural deceptions of our times. What lingering oppression of slavery remains, and how have I blinded myself to the evils of institutional racism? How has a global economy helped me, living in a country that consumes most of the world's resources, while hurting others in less fortunate circumstances? What other sins skulk in my soul, yet I am without the awareness or language to name them, let alone change them?

But God is always working, not content to leave us in our blindness. While Newton was in Charleston—a city influenced by George Whitefield's preaching on civility to slaves—the slave trader began writing letters and journal entries that showed pity for his human cargo. God was working in Newton's heart. Newton returned to England, married Mary Catlett, and . . .

Here again, I want the story to be different from what it is. I wish that Newton's emerging compassion for slaves would have saturated his heart, causing him to change careers and fight against slavery. But instead Newton squandered his money on the lottery and then embarked on another slave-trading journey, this time as captain of *The Duke of Argyle.* He began his travel log with the words "Journal of a voyage intended (by God's permission)."[33] More than a year later he returned home, having purchased and sold another two hundred human lives, read extensively on the Christian faith during his time ashore, and . . .

No, he still did not stop. He captained another ship, *The African,* on yet more slave voyages. Newton became a pastor to his crews, helping them see the grace of God, as his eyes remained mostly closed to the plight of the slaves the ship carried. The conditions of capture and transport were horrendous. Though more humane than most slave-ship captains, at times Newton resorted to torturing slaves to quell insurrections. Yet he wrote how being the captain of a slave ship was optimal for "promoting the Life of God in the Soul."[34] He could exert some control over the behavior of his crew, had ample leisure time for studying, was removed from temptations to waste time in social engagements, and could observe the majesty of God's creation. He regularly saw God deliver him from hazards of death.

Newton's slave trading might have continued for many more years except for a seizure that made a career change medically necessary. In all, Newton spent ten years trading slaves, most of them *after* reclaiming his Christian faith.

Newton's biography was not the story I expected, yet it is hauntingly familiar to the Christian journey we see in ourselves. Our disordered passions do not suddenly become ordered with a flash of insight or a spiritual awakening. Change is a lifelong calling, an epic journey. It was not until many years later that Newton could write, "[I] was blind but now I see."

How blind we all can be. So many prideful sins lurk beneath our awareness, stealing away the abundant life God desires for us and those around us. But God does not give up. "I am sure that God, who began the good work within you, will continue his work until it is finally finished on that day when Christ Jesus comes back again."[35]

Newton became a customs officer, studied theology, and eventually—despite feelings of unworthiness because of his past sins—became a minister at Olney, England, where he preached as many as a dozen sermons a week and often wrote a hymn a week.[36] He loved Mary faithfully, served his congregation and community well, and became an advocate for the abolition of slavery. Sometimes he annoyed parishioners because he seemed too gentle on sinners—perhaps because he saw the depths of sin in his past and was moved to extend mercy, as God had extended him such amazing grace: "Lord may I remember thy patience towards me when I drank down iniquity."[37] Newton believed that hearts are softened by the grace of the gospel, not by harsh accusation.

As Newton's eyes opened more fully with each passing year, he was horrified at his sin. One of his friends later recalled that he never spent thirty minutes with Newton without hearing the former captain's remorse for trading slaves. Newton called slave trading "a business at which my heart now shudders," and "a commerce so iniquitous, so cruel, so oppressive, so destructive."[38] It was always on his mind, nagging his conscience while reminding him of his utter dependence on God's forgiving grace. *Amazing grace—how sweet the sound—that saved a wretch like me.*

John Newton's pamphlet *Thoughts upon the African Slave Trade* played an important role in the political battles to end the slave trade. Two months before Newton's seventy-ninth birthday, after a major political victory for abolition, he wrote to a friend in Parliament: "Though I can scarcely see the paper before me I must attempt to express my thankfulness to the Lord, and to offer my congratulations to you for . . . your unwearied endeavours for the abolition of the slave trade, which I have considered as a millstone, sufficient, of itself sufficient, to sink such an enlightened and highly favour'd nation as ours to the bottom of the sea."[39] Bernard Martin, his biographer, concludes: "Above all, the life of John Newton demonstrates very clearly a *growth* of character; the only spiritual experience common to all."[40]

I once was lost but now am found, was blind but now I see.

When I began reading Newton's biography, I expected sudden enlightenment to come with his faith conversion on the stormy North Atlantic. I hoped the pride of his heart would suddenly be reversed, allowing him to love God and others above himself. How foolish my expectation! Sometimes I demand the same from myself and those I love: that our pride should suddenly be solved by a moment of insight, a spiritual renewal, or a commitment to change. How wrong this is. We are broken souls, struggling to see how our pride blinds us yet growing to see more clearly as God continues to work in our lives. Sight is a long process, calling us to a "long obedience."[41]

Seeing our pride problem occurs over a lifetime of pursuing God. Our vision is seldom restored in a single burst of light but with countless rays streaming into our darkened eyes over many years—and always in the midst of amazing grace. At the end of his life Newton said to his friends, "My memory is nearly gone; but I remember two things: That I am a great sinner, and that Christ is a great Savior."[42]

SIX

Blunted Minds

Jeremy McArthur thought he had a perfect plan. He rubbed his face with lemon juice, walked into two Pittsburgh banks in 1995 and robbed them in broad daylight. Of course the surveillance cameras recorded his every move, and he was quickly arrested after the tapes were aired on the eleven o'clock news. When he was arrested, Mr. McArthur was astonished: "But I wore the juice." He had the impression that having lemon juice on his face would make him invisible to the cameras. The newspaper article reporting this event was titled, "Trial and Error: They Had Larceny in Their Hearts, but Little in Their Heads."

Both our hearts and our heads are affected by sin. Disordered passions and dulled thinking are both part of the damage report. Alvin Plantinga explains: "Original sin involves both the intellect and the will; it is both cognitive and affective. On the one hand, it carries with it a sort of *blindness*, a sort of imperceptiveness, dullness, stupidity. . . . But sin is also and perhaps primarily an *affective* disorder or malfunction. Our affections are skewed, directed to the wrong objects; we love and hate the wrong things."[1]

In the previous chapter we considered how our passions are disordered, so that in our pride we love and hate the wrong things. Called to love God first, we end up loving self first; and called to love neighbor as self, we end up competing with neighbor in order to love self more. Our hearts are misaligned.

But pride affects more than just the heart. Pride also touches our minds. Our heads are as disarrayed as our hearts, making us vulnerable to all sorts of miscalculations, blunders, and sin.

One popular approach to understanding sin involves listing the sins that trip us up and then trying our best to resist those sins. Lists are not difficult to find in the Bible. The apostle Paul writes: "When you follow the desires of your sinful nature, your lives will produce these evil results: sexual immorality, impure thoughts, eagerness for lustful pleasure, idolatry, participation in demonic activities, hostility, quarreling, jealousy, outbursts of anger, selfish ambition, divisions, the feeling that everyone is wrong except those in your own little group, envy, drunkenness, wild parties, and other kinds of sin."2

Identifying and avoiding particular sins can be useful, but it is not enough. Notice the preface the apostle gives his list: "When you follow the desires of your sinful nature . . ." In other words, these acts of sin come from somewhere inside. We need to grasp our sinfulness, our broken condition, in order to understand the specific sins that plague us. Paul is instructing us to look for a deeper healing than we can ever find by keeping a moral to-do list. Early Christians understood this when they articulated the Seven Deadly Sins: pride, envy, anger, sloth, greed, gluttony, and lust. Notice that murder, genocide, adultery, orgies, and oppressing the poor do not even show up on the list. Are these not sins? Of course they are, but these early Christians understood what Paul was trying to say: our sins flow out of our sinfulness. The Seven Deadly Sins articulate the sin-stained condition of our hearts and minds, not an exhaustive list of all the bad things we might do. As Reformed theologian R. C. Sproul asserts, "We are sinners not because we sin. Rather, we sin because we are sinners."3

The early Christians—John Cassian and Gregory the Great, among others—put pride at the top of the damage report, the root from which all our sinfulness grows. If we want to grasp why sin matters, it is less useful to create a long list of sins and try to avoid them—what Dallas Willard refers to as the gospel of sin management—than to see the condition of our hearts and minds, confess our need for transformation, and reach out for God's healing grace. [4]

Pride taints our thinking as well as our affections. If we want to understand the grip of sin in our lives, we must understand the waywardness of our thoughts. I stand with centuries of believers before me, asserting that our errant thinking can be transformed by the grace of God, but first we must know that our thinking is fallible and often wrong. The purpose of rational discourse in the Christian tradition is to revolutionize our thoughts to better conform to the mind of God. We study Scripture, listen to sermons, read books, and seek counsel because we believe thinking is malleable. All throughout Scripture we see God reclaiming people's thoughts, instructing them to do justice, to love kindness, and to walk humbly with their God.[5]

> *If we want to grasp why sin matters, it is less useful to create a long list of sins and try to avoid them . . . than to see the condition of our hearts and minds, confess our need for transformation, and reach out for God's healing grace.*

Perhaps the greatest obstacle to transformed thinking is the very thing that makes our thinking faulty in the first place: pride. So we hide behind lemon-juice facials, not realizing how dulled our thinking has become and how desperately our minds need to be renewed.

➜ I THINK, THEREFORE I AM (OFTEN WRONG)

Heads are as paradoxical as hearts. Created in the image of God, we are blessed with many beautiful qualities; high among them is our capacity to reason. Our human ability to think should cause our jaws to drop in wonder of our spectacular Creator. We can reason, intuit, predict, and estimate in remarkable ways. Reasoning allows us to contemplate big ideas, to communicate them with one another, to test their validity and revise them accordingly. We can contemplate God's majesty and grace.

For centuries philosophers and theologians have discussed the marvel of human rationality, as celebrated by René Descartes's famous phrase, "I think, therefore I am." But because we place too much confidence in our reasoning, we often end up alone and isolated—churning through logic problems with illogical minds. Our thinking can draw us toward truth and toward others, or it can distance us from both if we swap the richness of community with the poverty of isolation. Our minds can deceive us, lead us astray, causing us to see worth in that which has no worth and to see error in the One who has no error. This is part of the damage report. It is part of our pride problem.

We have always had limits in our ability to think, even before sin entered the picture, because we are finite. But now we are both finite and fallen. The creation story suggests Adam and Eve fell into sin because they, as finite beings, wanted to know more than they were created to know. They wanted to be like God. The serpent's lie—that eating the fruit would allow humans to know as much as God—had the opposite effect. Searching for infinite knowledge, humans went from being clear but finite thinkers to being foggy finite thinkers. In the words of systematic theologian G. C. Berkouwer, "What actually happened is that by transgressing God's commandment the eyes of man were closed."[6]

Theologians discuss the noetic effects of sin, meaning that our intellect is dulled—our eyes closed—as a result of our fallen state.[7] In the narrow sense, the noetic effects of sin are that we cannot reason well enough to see our need for salvation. We do not perceive God, or our need for God, correctly. In our blindness, our dulled state of thinking, we cannot see the extent of our sin. Our only hope is found in God's grace. "God is so rich in mercy, and he loved us so very much, that even while we were dead because of our sins, he gave us life when he raised Christ from the dead. (It is only by God's special favor that you have been saved!) . . . God saved you by his special favor when you believed. And you can't take credit for this; it is a gift from God."[8]

In a broader sense, there are many noetic effects of sin. Our thinking is dulled in various ways because all creation has fallen from its initial state. In our prideful independence we fail to see how faulty our reasoning can be, and we end up with all sorts of problems.

The prodigal used his reasoning to plot his escape and had no intention of returning home. Having worked out a bright future in his mind, he took his money and ran. But with his fortune squandered, his future turned out to be as dull as his estate planning. He ended up alone, chatting with the pigs, wondering how he could have wandered so very far from home. In our pride we hold our own ideas above others' and ultimately find ourselves lonely, and often wrong.

> *Our thinking is dulled in various ways because all creation has fallen from its initial state.*

→ THE DEMON OF ERROR

I learned about Jeremy McArthur in an unlikely way: reading a professional journal article by two Cornell University scholars.[9]

These researchers use McArthur's story to illustrate the danger of being unaware of our incompetence. When we lack skill in some area of judgment, we probably also lack the ability to know we are not very good. <u>The worse we are at something, the greater the disparity between our actual abilities and our perceived abilities.</u> McArthur was not a good bank robber, but his bigger problem was that he lacked the skills to know that he was not a good bank robber. This is part of the damage report. Our dulled thinking keeps us from understanding our weaknesses.

It is not particularly upsetting that McArthur's incompetence landed him in prison for crimes he actually committed, but the same principle of dulled thinking can lead to horrendous social evils. One of the worst sins imaginable is killing a person for a crime he or she did not commit, but recent advances in forensic methods demonstrate that we have done this, or almost done this, many times. Randall Dale Adams, James Richardson, Henry Drake, and Anthony Silah Brown are among the hundreds of convicts who were exonerated before their execution. Dozens of others have not been so fortunate; they were innocent but were executed anyway.[10] Great social injustices begin with the pride of our hearts and our dulled thinking. If a prosecutor, judge, or jury lack the capacity to weigh evidence fairly, they also lack the ability to see they are being unfair. They may be completely confident— and yet completely wrong—in convicting a person.

On January 12, 2003, two days before leaving office, Illinois Governor George Ryan granted clemency to every inmate on death row in Illinois. One hundred sixty-four prisoners got their lives back and were given life sentences without the possibility of parole. In explaining his controversial decision, Governor Ryan pronounced the state's capital punishment system to be "haunted by the demon of error."[11] However one feels about capital punishment or Ryan's decision to grant clemency, he is correct about the demon of error. These errors are not demonic in a literal sense, but we are surrounded by a dark shroud of mistakes and miscalculations, and most often we are blind to our errors.

Transfer this principle to the world of everyday relationships. It's not just judicial systems that are haunted by the demon of error but every workplace, church, family, and person as well. How often do we cast judgment on another, thinking we know enough facts to be convinced of our personal verdicts, when actually we know very little of the situation? We bandage our incompetence with an extra layer of confidence as churches split, couples divorce, friends part ways, parents accuse children, and children rebel.

We are all prone to think poorly, and we fail to see our areas of incompetence. One husband is capable of experiencing and express-ing empathy, and another is not; but both think they are quite empathic. One wife has good nego-tiation skills, and another does not; but both believe they work things out well with their husbands. One friend listens well, and another does not; but both claim to be good listeners. The frightening thing is that we cannot know our areas of incompetence because if we lack the skills required to be competent, we also lack the skills to know we are incompetent. The only way we can see ourselves clearly is through the eyes of another. We need the wisdom to listen.

> *How often do we cast judgment on another, thinking we know enough facts to be convinced of our personal verdicts, when actually we know very little of the situation?*

Each of us is blinder than we know. Jeremy McArthur sits in jail pondering why he thought lemon juice would make him invisible. Others sit on death row for crimes they did not commit. The rest of us flounder in careers and relationships harmed by our own demons of error.

✦ PRESUMPTUOUS THINKERS

We are more confident than we are correct in our thoughts. Most all of us assume our thoughts are better reasoned, wiser, and more insightful than they really are. This premise built Las Vegas and Atlantic City. Gamblers assume that probabilities apply to other people, that their own hunches will work out and other people will lose their shirts. While Hollywood tells us to believe in ourselves, studies in the social sciences tell us that we already believe too much in ourselves. Psychologists call this the overconfidence phenomenon.

Overconfidence

An electrician convinces himself that he can change a simple breaker without turning off the main power supply, and he receives a life-threatening jolt of electricity as a result. A chemical engineer is sure there is no "product" in the supply line she needs to inspect, so she neglects to bleed the line before opening it. Severe chemical burns become the lifelong reminder of overconfidence. A former alcoholic goes to a bar with a friend, convinced he can withstand the temptation to drink, and once again he ends up in the claws of addiction. Every part of our human nature—including our reasoning—is less than it was created to be.

The pride of overconfidence wounds relationships. Maria and Christine, once dear friends, are now separated by the vast distance of overconfidence. Convinced that Maria and her husband, Jorge, were being too lenient with their two young sons, Christine confronted Maria, citing a few pithy Scripture verses and warning her of the damage being done by "sparing the rod." Marie erupted in anger: "How dare you tell me how to raise my children!" Things changed. They are still friends, but a pervasive tension now taints their time together. Maria feels uncomfortable because she hates feeling judged and criticized. Christine, deeply wounded by Maria's harsh words, feels misunderstood. Both are overconfident.

Maria and Jorge are sure they are raising their children well, show-ing the sort of kindness and understanding that neither of them experienced as children. They want something better for their chil-dren. Christine is certain that Maria's children are bound for a rebellious adolescence and that her words of confrontation were only meant to help her friend. She has seen lenient parenting back-fire time and time again. Both are sure they are right.

We live in a state of sin, a state in which our thinking is dulled with overconfidence, people are hurt, and relationships wounded as a result. It's the hum of the white noise, constantly reminding us that things are not right. Our thinking is a great gift, but when we trust it too much, we are vulnerable to foolish and costly errors.

Confirmation Bias

Overconfidence is bad enough, but it is particularly troubling when coupled with confirmation bias. That is, we actively seek information that confirms what we already believe. Most of us, when we walk into a bookstore, live out the confirmation bias as we head to a section of books that tend to confirm our beliefs. The Reformed theologian walks to the religion section to find books on Calvin, the postmodern mystic to the New Age section, the coun-selor to the self-help area, the financial analyst to the economic books. Then we pick up a few books and flip through the pages. If we like what we see, we conclude, "Oh, this looks like a good book," and we consider buying it. If we disagree with the author, we simply put the book back and conclude it is not worth our money. Rather than stretching ourselves and reading different perspectives, we look for books that confirm our ideas. After a while it seems as if "all the evidence" supports our beliefs, when actually we have failed to look at all the evidence. As a result, we are blind to contradictory evidence—plagued by the demon of error— and reluctant to change our minds even when we hold false beliefs.

Maria and Christine surround themselves with friends who confirm their beliefs. Shortly after Maria's confrontation with Christine, she and Jorge joined a church parenting class led by a like-minded couple. The class is filled with caring parents who eagerly find ways to nurture expressiveness and individuality in their children. The class is a great encouragement, affirming what Maria and Jorge already believe about effective parenting. Christine goes to a different church, also participates in a parenting class in which they are learning to raise children "God's way." Each week concurring parents gather and affirm the importance of firm discipline and clear expectations. Both Maria and Christine surround themselves with those who will confirm what they already believe, and their friendship remains ruptured.

Belief Perseverance
It gets worse. In addition to overconfidence and confirmation bias, there is the belief-perseverance phenomenon. We cling to our beliefs even in the presence of contradictory evidence. We are stubborn. Not only do we avoid contradictory information (confirmation bias), even when it is unavoidable and right in front of our eyes, we tend to discredit it so that we can cling to our prior beliefs (belief perseverance). We seem to hold our ideas until "death do us part."

"Don't confuse me with the facts." Political debates demonstrate belief perseverance. Politician 1 is given a question and presents a particular viewpoint. Politician 2 then discredits it with various statistics and arguments, at which point Politician 1 ignores Politician 2's arguments and holds on to the initial viewpoint. Then it is Politician 2's turn for a question, and the same thing transpires, but with roles reversed. When the debate is over, the commentators spin a story about who "won" the debate, mostly based on the politician who was most charming in resisting the other person's arguments (or perhaps based on which politician confirmed the commentators' prior beliefs). It would be death to a politician to say, "Oh, that is a very good point. I may be incorrect in some of my assumptions." Voters do not want intellectual honesty as much as charming intractability.

Sometimes Maria and Jorge notice that their children seem to be lost, looking for structure and guidance. At times their sons seem wild and out of control, less able than other children to constrain their impulses, and quite demanding. The parents dismiss what they see with trite reassurances: "Boys will be boys." "It's just the terrible twos." They persist in their permissive parenting, convinced they are right.

Sometimes Christine notices that her children lack joy and brightness. She sees amazing creativity and joy in Maria's sons. They smile, laugh, run, jump, and love life. Christine explains it away, saying, "They may seem happy now, but just wait until they are adolescents in the juvenile correction system."

> *The effects of our presumptuous thinking hinder our capacity to love one another well.*

Convinced they are right and impervious to contrary evidence, Christine and Maria continue in their beliefs. Both are partly right and partly wrong, but both think they are almost entirely right. The rift lives on.

We have three strikes against us—overconfidence, confirmation bias, and belief perseverance. The effects of our presumptuous thinking hinder our capacity to love one another well. Two people have differing viewpoints, both believe they are correct, both are overconfident in their perspectives, both can see only the evidence that confirms what they already believe, and both will persevere in their beliefs even when faced with conflicting evidence. No wonder it is difficult to resolve conflict in relationships! No wonder we so desperately need grace-filled relationships in which we can forgive and accept one another despite our differences. No wonder we need the transforming power of Christ in order to think of others as better than ourselves.[12]

Ian and Corrine were stuck in a negative cycle of overconfidence and stubbornness when they sought help for their marriage. Ian seemed distant to Corrine, who could sense his withdrawal into not only his work but also a friendship with a female coworker. The further away Ian seemed, the more Corrine grasped for him. She was trying to hold on to the man she loved, and she became demanding, controlling, and unpleasant in the process. Ian was trying to create greater independence in their relationship, and he became aloof, angry, and emotionally unavailable. The more Ian distanced himself, the more Corrine pursued. The more Corrine pursued, the more Ian distanced himself. Both were overconfident in their viewpoints. Ian insisted that his outside friendship was completely safe and that Corrine had no business interfering. Corrine was adamant that her concern was justified and that Ian had no right to invest himself in a close friendship with another woman. Both found evidence to confirm what they already believed. When Corrine found an unusually warm e-mail that Ian had written to his coworker, it proved to her that Ian was being foolish and emotionally untrue. It proved to Ian, who insisted the e-mail was within the bounds of friendship, that Corrine was out of control in her jealousy, snooping in his e-mails.

Both clung to beliefs that the other was wrong, even in the face of contradictory evidence: Ian had become too close to his coworker and had let his love for Corrine atrophy, but he could not see it. The e-mail was Exhibit A. It was not difficult for anyone (except Ian) to see his culpability. Corrine had become obsessed with her jealousy, pushing Ian away even as she was trying to hold on to him. Reading his e-mails without asking was Exhibit B. Her guilt was clear to others, but not to her. Both Ian and Corrine surrounded themselves with people who confirmed the beliefs they prized: Corrine with friends who voiced how foolish Ian was being, and Ian with friends who saw Corrine as overly controlling.

Slowly, and with a good deal of effort, Ian and Corrine were able to turn the negative cycle around before their story became more tragic. Both began to see how pride was blinding them from the truth. Corrine began to see how she was smothering Ian, driving him further away. Ian opened his eyes to his unfaithful heart and his foolish independence. They each began to change, slowly at first, encouraged by the changes they saw in one another. A negative cycle of defensiveness gradually evolved into a positive cycle of humility, confession of sin, forgiveness, and restoration. Confessing his sin of wandering off, Ian turned his heart and mind toward home, and Corrine offered forgiveness. Confessing her sin of attempting to control Ian, Corrine found healthy ways of giving Ian more space in their marriage, and Ian offered forgiveness. As long as they both thought they were right, they were doomed to conflict and misunderstanding. But as Ian and Corrine opened their eyes to the possibility of being wrong, they watched their marriage be transformed from pain into unexpected beauty.

One way to combat our presumptuous thinking is to actively search for ways we may be wrong, to deliberately look at things from another perspective and find the error in ours. We need to see our capacity for self-deception. We are sinners, broken in every way, and when we grasp this truth, we begin to see that others may be right and we may be wrong. If we listen closely, we hear the prodigal whispering, as he clings to his

> *We are sinners, broken in every way, and when we grasp this truth, we begin to see that others may be right and we may be wrong.*

father and abandons his presumptuousness: "I was wrong. I am so sorry. I don't know what I was thinking."

→ ERRANT THINKERS

Not only are we presumptuous, but we are often wrong in our thinking. Social scientists have described various sorts of thinking errors: we filter out important information while focusing in on selected details; we misconstrue things by using mental "shortcuts" based on what is most available in our memories; we create rigid mental stereotypes and then falsely interpret the world in light of our preconceived ideas; and we are vulnerable to making foolish choices when information is presented in a misleading context. In short, we are quick to make up our mind, often wrong, and easily manipulated.[13]

Marketers have taken our thinking errors to the bank.[14] One example is seen in the framing effect.[15] By presenting information in a particular way—framing it in a certain context—others can often shape our thinking to their pleasure. A major bank advertises its credit cards by instructing us to "live richly." The bank puts up billboards all over the country with messages such as, "Friends don't depreciate." The message is powerful: Use your credit card to make friends and enjoy life. The advertising campaign would be much less successful if the billboards presented the same message in a different way. Imagine a billboard that read: "Some fickle friends may hang around only if you spend money, and we will loan it to you for a moderately high interest rate so that you can attract this sort of friends." Or what if the slogan was "Pay us finance charges each month" rather than "Live richly"? Framing shapes the way we think.

Several years ago a well-known ice cream maker released a new "space-saver size" carton, presuming people would appreciate the extra space in their freezers rather than noticing they were buying 1.75 quarts of ice cream for the same amount of money as the older 2-quart container. If the information can be framed in a certain way, it will change the way consumers respond. The demon of error has a profit margin.

It is not an act of sin to be vulnerable to framing effects. Rather, it is evidence that we do not reason as carefully and logically as we think we do. It is part of the damage report—our thinking is not quite right. In our sinful, damaged state we are vulnerable to sinful choices, attitudes, and behaviors. The cost of buying a smaller carton of ice cream isn't so bad, but it is frightening to consider how we manipulate our minds to justify what we want to do. In essence, we use framing to justify our sin. The alcoholic says, "I can quit any time I want." The adulterer says, "My spouse has never provided for my emotional and sexual needs, so I found someone who would." The tax evader says, "Everyone cheats a little bit." The gossip says, "I just thought you should know"; the Christian gossip adds, "So you can pray about it." The materialist says, "I work hard, and I deserve it." The prodigal persuaded himself that he needed money and freedom to find a good life.

At first glance many of these thinking errors seem quite innocuous, but our pride is the catalyst that converts benign miscalculations into monumental and life-changing sin. An overworked man's commute takes him by a well-framed billboard advertisement for a new casino. This, plus his prideful overconfidence, begins the downward cascade that ends in a gambling addiction that cripples and devastates his

> *Our pride is the catalyst that converts benign miscalculations into monumental and life-changing sin.*

family. Our prideful capacity to think wrongly and to justify sinful choices is terrifying. Not only do we need others to help us think well, but we also need enough humility to accept what they have to say.[16]

➔ TUNNEL VISION

We need human community to think well, but we often shut others out just when we need them most. Though I have lived in the Chicago area for more than a decade, I make a regular habit of getting lost when driving unfamiliar roads. More than once Lisa has offered advice about where to turn or which exit to take, only to be met with, "Just be quiet for a moment so I can think." When will I learn that in the end it is often her advice that helps us find our way? In these moments of tunnel vision I shut out external distractions so I can think "better," and I end up thinking worse.

This sort of selective attention is helpful in some situations by allowing us to focus on the essentials and screen out external distractions. If you encounter an angry bear in the woods, you want to be able to concentrate on your next move. This would be a good time to think intently about freezing or running or playing dead or whatever it is you are supposed to do in times like these. It would not be a good time to get distracted with the beautiful sunset or the lovely wildflowers behind the bear's left foot or the buzzards circling in the sky. Similarly, selective attention allows a person to read a book without being distracted by the cat's scratching on the door or by the hum of the refrigerator.

Selective attention can be good, but it also can cause problems. We get in a good conversation and miss our bus stop or we watch television and forget that the cookies are burning or we focus on packing for the vacation and forget to turn off the iron. Sometimes it turns us into Lone Rangers in the moments when we need others to help us think well. I learned that all too painfully one year when Lisa and I took our three young children to a concert at a large state fair amphitheater. We arrived fifteen minutes before the concert started and were walking along the front of the amphitheater, looking for our seats near the stage. The seating scheme confused me, so I concentrated intently on finding our seats. Lisa was happy (even eager) to help, but I did the tunnel-vision thing: "Just let me figure this out." So I walked along as Lone Rangers do, holding five tickets in one hand and my oldest daughter's hand in the other, five paces in front of the rest of the family. As I studied the tickets, looking for the location of our seats, I did not notice when a clown tapped my daughter on the shoulder, removed her hand from mine, and inserted his two fingers into my hand instead. So there I was, walking along, studying concert tickets, holding a clown by the hand without knowing it. Unfortunately, the thousands of people in the stands above did know. I noticed the laughter and looked around to see what was happening. Then I realized they were laughing at me. And my family members, standing twenty feet behind me by now, were enjoying it quite a lot too. It was not my best moment.

Tunnel vision seems fairly innocent and innocuous in these examples, but it can also be malignant. How often do we, like the prodigal and Jeremy McArthur, get our minds set on a particular path to happiness and become so entrenched that we fail to see the frailty of our reasoning? We become overly focused on work, wealth, our bodies, a friendship, alcohol, a child's success, possessions, a spouse's approval, and we end up oblivious to the ways we are wounding others and loving them poorly. We emerge at the other end of the tunnel with addictions and obsessions, clinging to pride and to things that mean so little while leaving great treasures behind.

With tunnel-vision thinking we shut out others, naming them a distraction. In the end we end up thinking poorly and being alone. It is not a good combination because the more isolated we are, the more compromised our thinking becomes; the stranger our thinking becomes, the more we alienate others. We need others to fill in the gaps in our thinking, all the more so because we usually cannot see the gaps.

➜ A GIFT AND A CURSE

God made us as rational beings and gifted us with language and thinking skills unlike any found elsewhere in creation. But sadly, in our fallen state we are capable of exchanging gifts for curses. Our thinking errors reflect the intellectual dulling caused by our sinful state.

As I stood in the Hermitage Museum and pondered Rembrandt's rendering of the return of the Prodigal Son, I was struck by how well the artist had captured the curse of a misused gift. The father had made great sacrifices—both materially and emotionally—to grant the younger son his early share of the inheritance. The son was given an enormous gift that could be used for good or harm, but he exchanged a gift for a curse, wasting his resources as he dirtied

> *We need each other to help us think better than we might alone, and we need enough humility to admit our need for others.*

himself with depraved pleasure. He unwisely believed that his money would last forever, that the pleasure he bought would compensate for the morality he compromised, that his wild life was a better choice than the one he had left behind.

God has given us a great gift. A part of God's very nature has been granted us in the gift of thought. With thought we can understand God's majesty by studying the world around us. We can huddle together in human community and share the language of ideas. We can understand God's revealed Word. But we easily turn this gift into a curse with our shortsighted pride. We wander away, using the reasoning skills God gave us to construct arguments denying God's relevance. We squander the gift of thought on selfish ambition, trying to convince others that we are right rather than growing in wisdom by hearing what they have to say.

We ignore important peripheral information while clinging to that in the center of our vision. We hold fiercely to untenable beliefs even when they are clearly wrong, and we are more confident in our opinions than we ought to be. Instead of using our reasoning for good, we sometimes use it to distance ourselves from God's embrace and to seek false significance by asserting dominance over others.

This is not a call to retreat from thinking. Let's celebrate our capacity to think by studying, reading, reasoning, and engaging in rich and lively dialogue with others. But let's remember that our reasoning is part of our sinful state and thus vulnerable to error. We need each other to help us think better than we might alone, and we need enough humility to admit our need for others. And if we are humble enough—or if we become humble enough through the tragedies of life—our reasoning will help lead us down the dusty path and into the arms of the One who granted us this great gift in the first place.

SEVEN

{ *Noble Ruins* }

The story of this book is not new. It is the same story that reverber-ates through history, influencing every culture and every field of inquiry: medicine, humanities, philosophy, theology, social sciences, and art. It is, in the words of theological anthropologists, the story of humans as *noble ruins*. We are ruined by the effects of sin; we see our brokenness in every aspect of created order. The damage report is extensive. Yet we are noble, made in God's image and graciously deemed worthy of redemption. Augustine captured it well: "But in this river, as I may call it, or torrent of the human race, both elements are carried along together—both the evil which is derived from him who begets, and the good which is bestowed by Him who creates us."[1] If we sit long enough to listen and if we open our eyes wide enough, we hear and see the story of sin and redemption—the story of noble ruins—echoing in every corner of creation.

The Christian story is first a story about eternal redemption for those struggling in the mire of sin. "Because of God's tender mercy, the light from heaven is about to break upon us, to give light to those who sit in darkness and in the shadow of death, and to guide us to the path of peace."[2]

April knew about sitting in darkness. Raised on the mission field by devout parents, she was sent off to boarding school when she turned six, cast off to live seven hundred miles from her dad and mom. She lived among kind people, was treated well by her dorm parents, and enjoyed most of her peers. But April still felt an ache for home and a nagging sense of betrayal. How could these parents who claimed to love her send her so very far away? She recalled sobbing in her pillow at nighttime, a lonely little girl yearning for parents to hold and comfort her. She longed to escape the darkness.

Darkness makes us vulnerable. In her teenage years, after her family returned home from the mission field, April tried to find others to embrace her and take away the darkness. It didn't work. She slipped into a pernicious promiscuity that ravaged her relationships at home and undermined whatever self-confidence remained in her. The more she hated herself, the more she tried to fill the gaps in her soul with sex, wild parties, and all sorts of thrill-seeking. And still she sobbed in her pillow at night, alienated from her parents, disgusted at her choices, feeling desperately alone.

But residing in each of us—even in one so damaged by loss and sin as April—is a profound awareness that tells us we are worth saving. We may feel ruined by our own sins and the sins of others, but in the quiet recesses of our hearts we sense there is something worth saving. Even in the worst moments in life somehow we know that we are noble, created for love, and ultimately worth saving. Without some instinctual awareness of her intrinsic worth, April would have never cried out for help, never pursued counseling. But she did. April's task in counseling was to reclaim her nobility as she rebuilt her faith. Her life was marked by ruins, but she was a noble ruin.

With time, after slogging through layers of anguish and remorse, a light began to dawn in April's life. She expressed her pain to her parents, who surprised her with their humble repentance. She named her foolish adolescent choices and wept in contrition. On the other side of her tears April found the dawn of grace that expels darkness.

This is not just April's story—it belongs to each of us. Each of us has been wounded by the decisions and behaviors of others. We have complicated matters by our willful and sinful rebellion. We have sobbed—literally or figuratively—about the darkness in our souls as we grope for light. But the groping itself reveals hope. We would not cry out for help if there were not some inherent awareness that we are worth saving. So let's cry out boldly—in the harmony of human community, naming our sin and grieving our pain—and look expectantly for the dawn of grace.

We sat in darkness, in the shadow of death, until the light of heaven broke the great divide between God and us. We were lost in our sin, but God, in immense love, became human and dwelled among us. Through the incarnation, death, and resurrection of Jesus Christ, human sin has been named and forgiven. God and sinners reconciled. This ultimate gift of redemption is freely available to all who believe. The Christian story gives life and hope to countless souls around the world, and it is so powerful that it echoes through all creation.

> *So let's cry out boldly—in the harmony of human community, naming our sin and grieving our pain—and look expectantly for the dawn of grace.*

Listen to the story of the human body. It is invaded by influenza viruses and breaks down to a state of ruin, yet these are noble ruins, complete with immune systems. So the body heals. See and hear the story of art. Artists cause us to reflect on the pallid condition of our ruined souls with distorted images and cacophonies that disturb and provoke us, and yet they also amaze us with the beauty of creation through a painting, sculpture, poem, song, or photograph. Things around us and within us are crooked yet beautiful. Consider great literary classics. We call them great because they cause us to ponder the frail state of the human condition while inspiring hope that there is something noble to be claimed in every culture, time, relationship, and person. We are deceived and self-destructing, yet we reach for truth and are capable of great sacrifice, love, and goodness.

The story of sin and grace is timeless, and it is told over and over: when a wayward child returns home to a loving parent, when an estranged couple reconciles, when a homeless man finds shelter for the night, when a drug-addicted woman walks through the doors of a treatment center, when a soldier returns home from war, and when parents and lovers somehow find courage to move on when one does not return home from war.

The story is told every day, all around us. Sin and grace. Loss and redemption. Evil and good. Broken and beloved. Flawed but growing. Ruined yet noble.

Psychology tells the same story. An introductory psychology class my freshman year of college got me excited about the field I would eventually pursue as my career. The classes were relevant and interesting, and reading the textbook didn't put me to sleep (which speaks volumes to a sleep-deprived college student). Now, many years later, I still find psychology fascinating, though perhaps for different reasons. As I became interested in the language of sin, I began to see that in many ways psychology is the study of noble ruins.

This connection between psychology and sin is not immediately obvious because psychologists and psychiatrists rarely talk about sin. Of course there are exceptions, such as Karl Menninger's book *Whatever Became of Sin?* and O. Hobart Mowrer's indictment that psychologists have "cut the very roots of [their] being" by avoiding the language of sin.[3] Despite these exceptions, psychology has been silent on the topic of sin, especially the branches of psychology that pertain to counseling and psychotherapy. This is not just a mainstream psychology problem; it has affected Christian psychology as well. Philip Monroe, a faculty member at Biblical Theological Seminary, recently noted that only 43 of the 1,143 articles published in *Journal of Psychology and Theology* and *Journal of Psychology and Christianity* have been related to sin, and only four of those are related to the effects or treatment of sinful patterns.[4] I wonder if we lost the language of sin because the language of psychology took its place.

It is quite a paradox that psychology, a discipline that rarely discusses sin, can be helpful in fleshing out the stories of sin and grace that theologians and philosophers have been describing for centuries. Psychology is a broad discipline, ranging from biological sciences to psychotherapy, from prenatal development to death and dying, from parenting to social behavior. And every chapter of an introductory psychology text could be subtitled "Noble Ruins." Every chapter helps articulate the damage report.

➴ PROZAC AND THE PRODIGAL

One of the first chapters of most general psychology texts covers the nervous system. We could subtitle it "The Neurology of Noble Ruins."

The noble complexity of the human nervous system is astonishing, rendering the most convoluted intersections of our highway systems simple in comparison. I imagine that neuroscientists looking into their microscopes must have an experience similar to that of astronomers gazing into the sky on a clear night. The magnificence of creation is mind-boggling. It is God's masterpiece.

Think of a crazy traffic intersec-

> *It is quite a paradox that psychology, a discipline that rarely discusses sin, can be helpful in fleshing out the stories of sin and grace that theologians and philosophers have been describing for centuries.*

tion; it seems that most towns have at least one. In Glen Ellyn, Illinois, close to where I now live, the intersection of Geneva Road, St. Charles Road, and Main Street is called five corners, though I sometimes call it five minutes (the length of time one sits at the stoplight). However many corners you have in your town's most complex intersection, you know the routine. People avoid the intersection whenever they can, and if they cannot avoid it, they simply sit at the stoplight, suspended in time, wondering whoever conceived of such a disastrous meeting of multiple roads.

Now take the most complex intersection in your town and multiply it several billion times, and we get a faint glimpse inside the human nervous system. But in this case, no one is sitting at stoplights. Our 100 billion nerve cells and all the interconnections between them function like high-speed highways, but without tolls, traffic jams, stoplights, collisions, or road rage. We are wondrously made! Yes, our nervous system has a slow lane, with some smaller neurons transmitting their signals as slowly as two miles per hour, but the speed of other nerve cells is astonishing: as fast as two hundred miles per hour. Each nerve cell carries the signal and then hands it to the next, like a relay race. Small chemicals, called neurotransmitters, carry the message from one nerve cell to the next—they are the batons in this relay.

However, because our world is broken, the same neurotransmitters that transmit a nerve signal from one cell to the next can cause all sorts of problems. Too little of the neurotransmitter dopamine, such as in the case of Parkinson's disease, causes involuntary movement, learning and memory deficits, and emotional changes. Medicate people with Parkinson's too much, and they become paranoid because their brains will have too much dopamine, as is the case in patients with schizophrenia. Too much norepinephrine, and people might become manic and irresponsible; too little serotonin, and they may slump into depression. The delicate balance of the human nervous system is fragile and easily disrupted. God initially created humans with the perfect complement of proper neurotransmitters, but in a fallen world we live in imperfect bodies, which we take care of imperfectly. As a result, we end up with all manner of maladies and ailments. Add brain chemistry to the damage report.

Roberta sought help because of her clinical depression. Her days were filled with gloom, tears, and hopelessness. Waking early each morning, she tossed and turned as she dreaded the day ahead. She had lost her appetite, along with twenty pounds she could barely afford to lose. Because of the profound depth of her depression, I recommended she see a physician for antidepressant medication. She resisted, noting that leaders in her church saw depression as a spiritual problem that does not require medication.

I speak of Roberta, but this is a story that has recurred many dozens of times in my years as a psychologist. Do you see the fallacy here? By distinguishing between a spiritual problem and a medical intervention, her church leaders were assuming that our bodies and our spiritual lives are two distinct entities. They were able to see the immaterial effects of sin but not that sin tatters our bodies just as surely as it invades our wills. This is the age-old Gnostic heresy, to separate the spiritual from the material.

We are embodied souls, or ensouled bodies, making it untenable to neatly bisect the spiritual and the material parts of our being. Every part of us, even our neurotransmitters, are broken by the effects of sin. Roberta needed medication because she lives in a broken world where things are not the way they are supposed to be.

In mental health facilities all over the world we see the story of this book: sin meets grace, and broken people are restored. The depressed patient gets the courage to stagger to the psychiatrist's office, the psychiatrist listens, cares, prescribes Prozac (or any of several medications that affect serotonin levels), and refers the patient to a therapist. With time the depression lifts, and life looks bright again. Some people might object, noting that depression is not sin and Prozac is not grace. But look again.

The Prodigal Son put himself in a desperate situation through his sinful choices, making the connection between his sin and personal despair direct and easy to see. Depression is not sin in the same way, and much damage is done to those caught in the grips of depression when they are told that they brought on their own depression by sinful choices or by a lack of spiritual maturity. Drawing on the distinction made in chapter 3 between sinfulness, sins, and the consequences of sin, we can say that depression is not often the direct result of sins. However, depression does reflect our sinful state and the consequences of sin. In this sense sin and depression are closely linked—just as sin is closely linked with cancer and influenza and addiction. In a world without sin there would be none of these things. Depression reminds us that we live in a world that is not right, a world where the white noise is constantly humming, where people experience abuse and profound losses, where neurotransmitters are out of balance, where marriages flounder and die and leave children in the rubble, where material-ism seems to win and true spirituality seems to lose, where God is perceived as distant or irrelevant. Depression is a marker of the sin in our world and in our souls.

Prozac and psychotherapy may not seem like grace, especially in comparison with the forgiving embrace of the father in the story of the Prodigal Son, but they are tangible reminders of God's continual embrace of a humanity beset by sin. When a psychiatrist prescribes medication and a person's serotonin levels are changed as a result, this reveals God's common grace in a broken world. God is always working—in the pharmaceutical research lab and in houses of worship, in the therapist's office and the pastor's study, in the psychology text and in the devo-

tional reading—redeeming that which is broken, offering us
water for our thirst and food for our hunger. When a psychologist provides psychotherapy or a pastor offers counsel and a
person begins feeling better, we can celebrate God's active,
sustaining presence in creation. Many marriages and families
thrive without a need for counseling services, which also reflects
the goodness of Creator and creation. Common grace is embracing us everywhere. We are surrounded by God's favor.

Throughout my years as a psychotherapist I have come to realize
that I am not so much doing my own work as I am participating
in God's natural rhythm of healing. It's not that people get better
because I am applying the proper
techniques from cognitive therapy
or choosing just the right words to
say at strategic moments. People
get better in the context of meaningful relationships. Indeed, the
research literature is clear and
compelling: psychotherapy is
effective, and most forms of
psychotherapy work equally well
for most problems. Except for a
few highly specific disorders, such
as panic disorder, no one therapy
stands head and shoulders above
any other. This has caused some to
suggest that common factors
account for the success of psycho-
therapy. Good therapists create effective relationships in which
intimate details of life can be discussed, and they care for a person
in times of need. Effective therapists are empathic and genuine in
their concern for those seeking their help. In short, they emulate

> *God is always working—
> in the pharmaceutical
> research lab and in
> houses of worship, in
> the therapist's office and
> the pastor's study, in the
> psychology text and in
> the devotional reading—
> redeeming that which is
> broken, offering us water
> for our thirst and food for
> our hunger.*

something like grace. People come to a therapist in a broken state, and the therapist reminds them they are noble ruins. Most therapists do this without knowing they are doing God's work, but it is still God's work.

✦ HUMAN VELCRO

Another chapter in most general psychology texts covers human development. It could be subtitled "A Lifetime of Noble Ruin."

The nobility of creation is stunning: a heart that beats within six weeks of conception; bonding that immediately and instinctively occurs between parent and child; the acquisition of language, reasoning, and moral character; the young adult's drive to mate and generate new life; the midlife desire to pursue excellence in meaningful work; and the social connections of retirement years. It is no surprise that Harry Blamires, author of *The Christian Mind,* concludes that "the Christian's conception of the human person is a high one, his sense of sacredness of human personality being deeply grounded in revealed theological truth."[5] We see God's rational and relational image embedded in human nature, and it gives us cause to worship a good Creator.

Those who have birthed or adopted a child, or witnessed a birth, recognize the nobility of new life. With the birth of each of our three daughters, Lisa and I reveled in the beauty and goodness of created life. We nestled these little noble ones in our arms, staring into their eyes as we exploded with gratitude. Almost every parent knows the power of these first moments of the parent-child relationship—life's priorities settle into proper perspective as love wells up and overcomes us. The nobility of new human life is a given; parents intuitively know this child has boundless value.

Yet in human development we see both the noble and the ruins: the fetus whose heart stops beating because of profound genetic defects; the orphan who fails to thrive because there is no adult providing emotional care; the person who cannot develop language because of pervasive developmental disorders; the crisis of aloneness in adulthood; the heartache of sterility; life's drudgery for those unable to find meaningful work; and the despair of isolation that some face in life's sunset years.

An important advance in human development is found in *attachment theory,* which comes from the work of John Bowlby, an English psychoanalyst and research scientist who was influenced by Konrad Lorenz, an ethologist who studied imprinting in animals.[6] Bowlby developed important ideas about human instincts for attachment, demonstrating how we are hardwired for connection. From the moment of birth we are human Velcro.

Even in the first days of life an infant is drawn to the parent, and the parent to the child. When nursing infants move their eyes, checking out various parts of the new world around, their eyes consistently come back to the One True Thing—the mother's eyes. At birth, infants' visual systems are optimized for distances of about twelve inches. Not coincidentally, this is the same distance from the mother's breast to her eyes. Eye contact builds connection, and human infants seem to know this as instinctively as a baby bird knows to break out of a shell. Complex biological phenomena occur during these early days of attachment as well. Both infant and mother are instinctively falling in love, gazing at one another, attaching from the first moments of life. The miracle of attachment continues throughout life.

A two-month-old infant is cooing happily in the crib with the parent nearby. The parent leaves for a moment, maybe to answer the telephone or check on something in the kitchen. What happens? Those gentle coos are gradually transformed into dissatisfied whimpers and eventually to earsplitting screams. We normally think that it is the parent who trains the child, but what if it is the other way around? At least in this case the child is training the parent. "When you stay here, I will reward you with pleasant coos, but when you leave me alone, I will punish you with whimpers and screams." This is not the deliberate willful choice of a two-month-old but instinctual behavior woven into the fabric of human life. We are social creatures looking for connection. Babies reach out for attachment, and if that doesn't work, they cry out until someone hears.

As the child grows, the desires for attachment persist. Two-year-olds play independently with Lego blocks, crayons, and kitchen pans, but every few moments they pause and go check with the parent, as if to say, "Are you still here? Do you still care about what I am doing?" The desire for autonomy is balanced with the lifelong quest for attachment.

As humans grow older, they become more sophisticated, of course, but attachment is a lifelong theme. When I left home and drove a thousand miles away to a college campus I had never seen before, I didn't arrive with nagging doubts about textbooks, library hours, and course requirements. No, my mind was on social connections. *What will people think of this farm boy from Oregon? Will I make friends? Will I like my roommate? Will he like me?* The first task of college was to find friends, and then I could settle down and concentrate on my studies.

It is good and right that we seek attachment. God is relational, and as a relational being, God lovingly created us to be relational. What a gift to be in relationship with others, whether it's the nursing infant finding its mother's eyes to be the One True Thing or the couple celebrating their golden wedding anniversary. We are made for relationship, made to be noble.

But we are noble ruins. Sadly, attachment is not always healthy in our sinful world. Some children have attachment disorders, situations in which they are incapable of attaching with their caregivers. Other people form unhealthy attachments, and their lives are marked by anxiety, fear, ambivalence, or withdrawal.

Nina longed for relationship, as all of us do. She yearned for a

connection with her workaholic father, but he was nowhere to
be found. She wished for a close, confiding relationship with her
mother, but she received her mother's harsh criticism instead.
Now launched into her adult world, Nina has watched three of her
marriages come and go—each with stories of abuse and unfaithful-
ness. Her lifelong quest to fill the relational gaps from her childhood is not working out well.

Nina, or someone in similar circumstances, can be found in counseling offices all over the world. Our instincts for attachment and the
wounds of living in a sinful world so often meld into shattered dreams.

Attachment has beautiful connotations when thinking of a child
and parent bonding during the first days of life or when celebrating
a happy wedding anniversary, but it is less appealing for the fly
attached to flypaper. Our attachments can be beautiful and noble
or they can be painful and destructive.

Our human capacity for attachment is viewed positively in
contemporary psychology but often as a burdensome concept by
spiritual writers through the centuries. These spiritual writers
remind us how we are prone to form false attachments that lead
us away from our deepest longings and needs.

Attachment makes us vulnerable to counterfeit pursuits: those
that claim to satisfy our deepest needs but end up being a cheap
substitute. Speaking of these counterfeits, the Old Testament
prophet Isaiah queried, "Why spend your money on food that does
not give you strength? Why pay for food that does you no good?
Listen, and I will tell you where to get food that is good for the
soul!"[7] We might ask the same today: Why do we attach ourselves
to that which means so little while disregarding our soul's deep
yearning for God? How often do we elevate a hobby, a friend, a
habit, a job, or a ministry goal to a place of central importance in
our lives, attaching to it as if it were our ultimate pursuit? Attachment becomes addiction.[8] We are not only human Velcro, ready

to form good and meaningful relationships, but we are indiscriminate Velcro, inclined to attach to all the false things as well as the true things. False attachments pull us away from God's design for our lives. From a monastery in New York on Ash Wednesday of 1979, Henri Nouwen cried out to God: "There is so much in me that needs to die: false attachments, greed and anger, impatience and stinginess. O Lord, I am self-centered, concerned about myself, my career, my future, my name and fame."9

Nouwen's words strike with poignancy and relevance as he interweaves false attachments with a description of pride. We so easily build idols of the heart, clinging to the wrong relationships—or to the right relationships for the wrong motives—or using our attachments to people to avoid our deeper yearning for God. Or perhaps we give up on people and God altogether and slip into the world of attachments to things: investment accounts, cars, cocaine, reputations, gambling, houses, careers, sex, or alcohol. Saint John of the Cross, a sixteenth-century Carmelite monk, noted that false attachments "weary, torment, darken, defile and weaken [the soul]."10

> *We are not only human Velcro, ready to form good and meaningful relationships, but we are indiscriminate Velcro, inclined to attach to all the false things as well as the true things.*

In 1896 George Stratton developed a pair of prism glasses that turned the world upside down. Not the way we normally think about turning the world upside down today—Stratton didn't write a best-seller, develop a new computer operating system, break a scoring record, or develop a theory of quantum mechanics. His prism glasses literally turned the perceptual world upside down. When wearing these glasses, he saw ceilings as floors and floors as ceilings. At first this was terribly disorienting because humans constantly use visual cues to guide motions. Stratton would try to reach up, but his hand would appear to go down. He tripped and fell frequently. At first he was nauseous and disoriented. But a strange thing happened over a period of days. Gradually Stratton became adjusted to his upside-down world. His hands began to accommodate to the changes; soon he could pick up a glass of water and quench his own thirst. He stopped tripping, and the nausea went away. His visual world was still upside down, but his brain had adapted to the inverted world so that he could function almost normally.

We do the same thing with our attachments. We take something that is false, turn it upside down, and make it look true. And after we do it long enough, it begins to seem normal. Our appetites, distorted by life in a sinful world, make us prone to the prism lenses of moral deception.

Our capacity to attach is a beautiful gift from our good Creator, allowing us to enter into meaningful connections from the earliest moments in life. These connections reflect our nobility—we are made in the image of a relational God. But we are sinful and ruined nobility, constantly struggling to orient ourselves. Our false attachments so easily capture our passions and lead us away from God and meaningful human community.

✦ PARENTING: A TAPESTRY OF SIN AND GRACE

Somewhere in the human development chapter of the general psychology text we will find a section about parenting styles. It could be subtitled "Parents as Noble Ruins."

Some noble part of us emerges when we have children. Until I became a parent for the first time, I didn't know some layers of my personality existed: a profound

> *Our false attachments so easily capture our passions and lead us away from God and meaningful human community.*

capacity to love as fathers do, a desire to protect, and a yearning to know and nurture my children. It was a paradigm shift. Part of God's image awoke in me, reminding me that God's goodness is revealed in this human form of mine. And then the next twenty-two years of parenting provided daily reminders that I am a noble ruin.

Researchers studying parenting styles have confirmed what all of us who are parents intuitively know: Finding proper balance in parenting is like walking a tightrope. Parents who slip too far to the extreme of permissiveness raise children who are prone to irresponsibility and who show little regard for others. Permissive homes have few rules or expectations, people come and go as they wish, and children often flounder because they lack defined boundaries and time together with other family members. But if we slip too far the other way—toward authoritarianism—we risk raising children who are timid, unsure, and secretive. Authoritarian parents are rigidly controlling, insisting on absolute obedience without negotiation. Children in these homes eventually stop asking why because they tire of hearing, "Because I told you so." In the middle we find that ideal balance of the authoritative parent who is strong and consistent yet responsive, caring, understanding, and willing to negotiate. Healthy parenting reflects our noble capacity to lead and to listen. It sounds fairly straightforward, but every parent knows better.

Lisa and I are recent empty nesters and often reflect on our years of parenting. When they were young, we would sneak in our children's rooms after they fell asleep and watch them sleep. Thinking of them now, recalling the indescribable feeling that swelled in my soul as I watched them sleep is as close as I can get to understanding how much God cares for us. The apostle Paul describes it this way in the New Testament: "May you have the power to understand, as all God's people should, how wide, how long, how high, and how deep his love really is. May you experience the love of

Christ, though it is so great you will never fully understand it. Then you will be filled with the fullness of life and power that comes from God."[11]

Sometimes at night, as I am falling asleep, I picture God watching over me, swelling with love for me, a beloved sinner. In God's eyes we are noble, loved beyond measure.

But unlike God's love for me, my love for my daughters is stained with sin. In those moments watching them sleep, I experienced a profound awareness of how unconditional my love could be. I could not imagine anything stopping me from treating my daughters with kindness, mercy, and grace. But when they would wake up each morning, I did not always treat them as one who loves unconditionally. There were many times that I wished for an Undo button in parenting, like the kind we have in word processors and electronic spreadsheets. I remember the glances of disapproval, the harsh words, the moments when some preoccupation in my mind seemed more important than truly listening, and the standards of perfection that deflated their best efforts. We also experienced many moments of grace in our home as Lisa and I extended compassion, care, and forgiveness throughout our daughters' childhood years. And our children did the same for us, forgiving their imperfect parents and straining to see the best in us. Every home in every time and culture weaves a complex tapestry of sin and grace.

➜ ON AND ON

The human nervous system, attachment, and parenting are just a few examples of topics we might find in a psychology text. Each demonstrates our condition as noble ruins. We are created and loved by a gracious God, wondrously made, but soiled by the brokenness of our fallen creation and the sin embedded deep in our hearts.

Many more examples can be found in the pages of a psychology text. If read through the eyes of theology, the text is—page after page—a damage report.

The chapter on learning demonstrates how we are made to respond to orderly laws of reinforcement, and yet these same laws keep us in patterns of self-destruction as well as patterns of health. So the laws of learning may keep some people driving the speed limit, exercising, taking out the trash, and showing up for work on time, but these same laws cause others to overeat, gamble too much, drink too much, and spend more than they earn.

The chapter on psychopathology shows how our bodies are created with amazing alarm systems to mobilize us in dangerous situations, and yet for many people the alarm system goes off unnecessarily and creates all manner of havoc. It is wonderful to have our alarm system when we need to run for our lives to get out of a burning house, but it's a nuisance when the same alarm goes off without provocation in the subway or the grocery store. Those who suffer from panic attacks know the nuisance of false alarms.

We are noble ruins, broken and beloved.

The social influence chapter demonstrates that we are made as social creatures, naturally drawn to human communities. Our social connections allow us to form deep and meaningful friendships and caring organizations. But these same prosocial tendencies make us bend the truth in order to fit in. So we easily fall to peer pressure, failing to stand up for our beliefs when they go against the social tide.

The cognition chapter teaches that we are thinking beings, working hard to analyze and compute and figure the facts of life. So we build bridges that don't collapse and write computer programs and invent medical treatments. And yet our thinking is prone to error, and in the psychopathology chapter we see how our thoughts turn against us as we talk ourselves into depressive slumps and angry tirades.

Human memory is the topic of another chapter. Memory is an incredible gift, allowing us to recall the aroma of our grandmother's apple pie, the smells of the junior high locker room, songs from the senior prom, and the grammar rules learned in third grade. But our memories are not as reliable as we think. When we have gaps in our memories, we fill them in with fabrications, and then we cannot tell the difference between real and fabricated memories. In fact, we falsely assume all memories are real.

Physical attractiveness is a gift that draws people together, as discussed in the social perception chapter. We long for beauty and find beauty in one another, and yet we do so in a biased and unfair way. Highly attractive people are viewed more positively than less attractive people; they are seen as more intelligent, are more likely to be hired, and they are treated better.

The list could go on and on. We are noble ruins, broken and beloved.

→ STRAYING AWAY, STAYING AWAY

Like the Prodigal Son, we are both noble and ruined. In our ruined state we inevitably stray from home. Our hearts are deceitful and sinful, so we take the many blessings given us and wander away to faraway places where we can squander our resources and indulge ourselves in materialism, overuse of alcohol, obsessive work, sexual addictions, self-pity, sloth, numbing entertainment, narcissism, or any number of other vices. Some people wake up, smell the pigsty, and decide it is time to go home. Others stay away, refusing to turn back to a place of mercy and forgiveness.

Sometimes I have stayed away because I cannot grasp my ruined state. "I'm OK," I insist. "I am doing fine." My problems are recast as someone else's intrusion in my life or as the lack of support I am receiving. And as long as I convince myself this is so, I stay away, blind to the healing arms awaiting me.

At other times we stay away because we fail to see our noble state. We see ourselves as too far gone, too depraved, too damaged, too despicable to show our faces around home again. And so we stay away, feeding the pigs, bemoaning our fate, and despairing about the future.

The prodigal saw himself as a noble ruin. Nouwen writes: "On the one hand the younger son realizes that he has lost the dignity of his sonship, but at the same time that sense of lost dignity makes him also aware that he is indeed the *son* who had dignity to lose."[12]

The son saw himself as ruined enough to need help from his father and noble enough to suspect his father would take him back, at least as a hired servant. So he wiped the pig slop from his hands, turned around, and headed home.

PART THREE

HEADING
HOME

EIGHT

{ *Homeward Bound* }

Home. For me it was a house my grandfather built on forty-five acres in Oregon, where my family grew hazelnuts and walnuts. Yes, I am a psychologist who grew up on a nut farm. It wasn't a perfect place. As an adult I have grown into some understanding of how much pain and dysfunction were contained inside those farmhouse walls. But it was home: the place where I learned to twirl in circles until I fell down dizzy on the green shag carpet. People bought seriously shagged carpet back in the 1960s, the kind that my mother used to rake with a garden tool to keep the pile standing upright. We worked hard in my home. We laughed some and probably didn't cry as much as we should have. We watched television and wrestled playfully on the floor and ate dinner together. In our broken sort of way we loved each other. When I went away—whether for a day at Harvey Clarke Elementary School or a week at summer camp or a semester at college—I returned home time and time again. It was the place where I learned love. My mother, like her mother before her, showed an amazing capacity to love. Whatever capacity I now have to love, I owe mostly to those two women.

My home is gone now. The house is still there nestled in the midst of those hazelnut and walnut trees, but someone else lives there. I don't know their names. My parents limped along in a difficult marriage, fairly well at times, for almost forty years before calling it quits. I still enjoy them both, but I can no longer visit them at the same time now that they live apart. My sister and I e-mail sometimes, and call even less; we see each other only about once a year because I live more than two thousand miles away. We were once four souls living in a farmhouse with ugly shag carpet, and now we are scattered about—each with an unresolved longing for home.

Except in some tragic situations, home is a place where we learn love. We don't learn it perfectly, of course, because all human love is sin-stained. But however flawed home's love may have been, it is a powerful force that calls us by name day after day and dream after dream. Love calls us home. The power of home called to the prodigal at the pigs' feeding trough, drawing him back to a place of love and security. For most of us, if we slow down and quiet down long enough, we hear the call to come home. We may be adept at drowning out the call with the clatter of Wall Street, the verbal haze of the ivory tower, the zeal of ministry, or the busyness of parenting, but in moments of quiet reflection or at nighttime when we cannot censor our dreams, we still hear the quiet call to come home.

Going home is a spiritual journey. All the rest—farmhouses, wrestling on the floor, twirling in circles, and the security of married parents—is a metaphor that helps us connect with the great spiritual hope of living and dying: going home. Our homes in this world serve to remind us that we are made for something beautiful, a place where we are surrounded by perfect security and love and goodness. Our delightful moments of repose and laughter and reflection here bear a faint resemblance to the home we are created to enjoy but have never fully known. Like all journeys, the journey home has a beginning, middle, and end. Because our heavenly journey often turns things upside down and inside out—first and

> *Love calls us home.*

last, greatest and least, strength and weakness—we begin by considering the end of the journey.

➔ HOME, WHERE OUR HEART IS

We journey because we believe there is a destination; we are homeward bound. Turning back from the pigpen and heading home is a journey of hope, believing something good awaits us at the end of the pilgrimage. Whatever obstacles and challenges we face on the journey home are viewed in light of the ultimate destination. As the apostle Paul writes in the New Testament, "For our present troubles are quite small and won't last very long. Yet they produce for us an immeasurably great glory that will last forever!"[1]

Whether we know it or not, we were created for something far more beautiful and magnificent than what we experience in this sin-contaminated existence. We instinctively yearn for home. Mark Buchanan, a pastor who dares to dream about heaven, puts it this way: "We're heaven bent. . . . our hearts have an inner tilt upward. . . . the grain of our souls leans heavenward."[2]

In heaven our sin will cease, and grace will overwhelm us. Can you imagine a time when we no longer struggle with living in a sinful world? Picture the pure freedom to choose rightly. Imagine the joy of thinking and caring as much about others as we think and care about ourselves. Envision the absolute forgiveness for the sins of the past and the purity of life without self-centered distortions and distractions. All the white noise will be transformed to perfect tranquility, and we will no longer be surrounded by reminders of our sinful state. I imagine a body with no lower back pain, a place where friends won't be getting cancer, where we won't have to fear being authentic with others because every fiber of our being and theirs will be good and every motive pure. I picture a world free of heart disease and aging and those little hairs that grow out of our ears after we turn forty. I imagine a place of unblemished beauty and glorious music, of perfect love, of finally being able to slam-dunk a basketball. I envision a place where every counseling center and divorce attorney and child protection agency will be out of business, where the makers of ibuprofen and Prozac will have no market, and where no one will have to fight with an HMO or scrounge through a Dumpster for food. Every tear will be wiped away, and mourning will be exchanged for rejoicing.

And I imagine how all that, as beautiful as it is, will fade into insignificance as we meet the One who has always loved us with a flawless, gorgeous love. We will collapse on our knees as prodigals with tattered sandals and broken hearts at the end of an arduous journey, and we will fall into the arms of everlasting grace. Merciful kindness expressed to us who do not, who cannot, deserve it. We will be home.

> *We will collapse on our knees as prodigals with tattered sandals and broken hearts at the end of an arduous journey, and we will fall into the arms of everlasting grace.*

Sometimes I find a quiet place to sit and absorb beautiful songs about heaven: Chris Rice's "Deep Enough to Dream," Fernando Ortega's "Beyond the Sky" and "Give Me Jesus," and Sandi Patti's and Wayne Watson's "Another Time, Another Place," and others.

I close my eyes, allow myself to be surrounded with stereophonic hope, and breathe in the indescribable joy that lies ahead.

➜ A SORT-OF METAPHOR

Our journey toward heaven is not a metaphor. Christians believe it is a literal destination for those accepting God's gift of grace. We believe heaven is a surety, something that anchors us with hope and direction. But there is also an uneasy, sort-of metaphor embedded here. It is "uneasy" and "sort-of" because using heaven as metaphor could so easily undermine the *reality* of heaven that awaits us.

Heading home will ultimately be fulfilled in eternal glory, but don't we also turn and head home throughout our lives? Isn't there a small taste of heaven each time we turn away from sin and embrace God's good for our lives? When the wayward adolescent confesses wrongdoing, turns around, and heads home, we see God's presence here in this broken world. Sort of like what heaven will be. When the angry spouse's heart is broken in contrition and a tender love renewed, we see a faint glimpse of heaven. When the work-addicted adult repents for being an absent parent and turns toward a smaller home—because the big one needs to be sold— we feel an inner swelling of hope that reminds us that God is preparing a mansion for us. When, in the midst of an argument, we strain to see how we are being selfish and unreasonable and turn toward true listening and reconciliation, isn't it because the work of God is reaching down to us, reminding us that a better day is coming? When, knowing that our wills are weak, we turn away from temptation and choose to do right, we remember that the glimmer of sin is fleeting and the joy of home eternal.

I recall the mingled feelings of terror and grief a pastor friend experienced when he was arrested for a publicly disgracing misde- meanor. It not only brought incredible shame to him and his family but also resulted in great losses: his job, many of his friends, his wife's confidence in him, his support system at church, the trust of his children. It was a terrible time in his life, a horrifying time for his family. Some time later Lisa and I were having dinner with this couple, enjoying a summer evening on their back patio, when they told us how God was working in the worst time of their lives. Despite all the losses the arrest and ensuing media attention brought, at least the years of secrecy and duplicity were being confronted. My friend had named his sin, begun to look honestly at layers of brokenness in his life, and asked his wife for forgiveness. She was facing her fear, anger, and insecurity and beginning the long journey of healing. They both faced enormous pain and many challenges in the months and years ahead, but they were guided by the hope that comes when we turn from our sins and head toward home.

➔ THE FIRST STEP

With a glorious home in sight, our spiritual journey begins with a single step: admitting our sin. In our postmodern era we have many spiritualities swirling around us. Christian spirituality is distinct from the others at many points, but the differences in this first step are utterly profound. Christian spirituality is not so much about finding ourselves as it is admitting our inability to find ourselves. It is not so much about searching inwardly for truth as it is admitting our inner weakness and looking outwardly for a transcendent God who is Truth. In the Christian story the devastating cost of sin is paid by the incarnation, atoning death, and resurrection of Jesus Christ. "God so loved the world that he gave his only Son, so that everyone who believes in him will not perish but have eternal life. God did not send his Son into the world to condemn it, but to save it."[3]

Christian spirituality is not so much about finding ourselves as it is admitting our inability to find ourselves. It is not so much about searching inwardly for truth as it is admitting our inner weakness and looking outwardly for a transcendent God who is Truth.

Admitting our sin and brokenness, our need for the intervening work of Jesus, is the beginning point of Christian spirituality. Roy Hession in *The Calvary Road* writes: "To be broken is the beginning of revival. It is painful, it is humiliating, but it is the only way"[4] Nouwen, in writing to a friend (letters that were later published as *Life of the Beloved*) writes: "You are a broken man. I am a broken man, and all the people we know or know about are broken. . . . It is often difficult to believe that there is much to think, speak or write about other than our brokenness."[5] The journey of Christian spirituality begins with confronting our sinful state, our brokenness, our need. As we glimpse our sin, we begin to see the enormous pain we have caused God, others, and ourselves; utter brokenness is the only reasonable response. There is no other way to begin the Christian spiritual journey.

Barbara Brown Taylor, an Episcopal priest, argues compellingly that we have exchanged a Christian language of sin for two alternative vocabularies.[6] One alternative is a medical vocabulary in which people are viewed as sick rather than sinful. If we are sick, then we need treatment. Clearly there is value to this vocabulary, and people often need treatment for sickness. But if we reduce all human problems down to sickness, then we miss the riches of confession, grace, and redemption. Taylor suggests this is the error of Christian liberalism.

A second alternative is the language of the legal system. In this vocabulary we are guilty of crimes and in need of punishment. Again, there is value to this vocabulary. Some people commit crimes, and sometimes punishment is right. But if the human problem is reduced to crime, we again miss the riches of grace and redemption. Such a view of sin points fingers, elevates one sinner above another, and ultimately destroys the power of the Christian message and the appeal of Christian community. Taylor suggests this is the error of Christian fundamentalism.

It is time to return to a vocabulary of sin. Some people are sick, and some are criminals, but we all are sinners. By acknowledging sin, we choose the path of Christian spirituality and introduce the hope of turning from our prideful ways, of confessing how we have hurt God, others, and ourselves, and of seeking grace. All of us are profoundly scarred by the sin of others, and we have wounded others deeply with our sin. Yet God is constantly working, always redeeming the broken places in our lives, calling us home. Admitting our sin is the first step of the Christian's spiritual journey.

At the beginning of the comedy *What about Bob,* the neurotic hero of the movie, Bob Wiley, rubs his temples and repeats, "I feel good, I feel great, I feel wonderful." He has learned a therapeutic language to assuage his angst, but it is clearly superficial and weak. Is it possible that this caricature of therapy is rooted in truth? Have we exchanged the language of sin with the language of pop psychology? Have we psychotherapists invested so much in shallow models of symptom reduction that we have overlooked a greater opportunity for healing and growth? Have we been swept away with the *I'm OK—You're OK* Zeitgeist when it would bring greater peace and hope to acknowledge what a mess we all are?

Early in my career I met with a man for six months to help him with his depression. We evaluated his self-talk and made some systematic adjustments to the way he looked at himself and others, and ultimately he started feeling much better. Several months after he finished treatment, I learned that he had sexually abused his niece for several years when she was a child. I pondered my therapeutic intervention, and though it may have been of some use to him, I think that I missed something much more important. I suspect he came to my office longing for a place where he could confess and enter the long spiritual process of repentance and restitution; perhaps he even hoped for forgiveness and reconciliation. This man yearned for the kind of authentic connection with a therapist that emulates a sinner's cry for God: "Give me the courage and freedom to appear naked and vulnerable in the light of your presence, confident in your unfathomable mercy."[7] He longed to be the prodigal and for me to be the father. What he got instead was altered self-talk: "I feel good, I feel great, I feel wonderful." One could argue that this is just an example of bad therapy, and it may be, but it was what I had been trained to offer. The therapeutic systems that I learned in graduate school and in my postdoctoral training do not use a language of sin and therefore do not provide opportunities for confession, brokenness, redemption, and grace.

Sometimes I wonder about this man's niece. What sort of scars does she live with every day because of his sinful choices? I imagine what a beautiful gift it might have been for her to have her uncle speak words of repentance: "I don't know if you can ever forgive me for what I did, and I realize my sin makes it unreasonable to have any sort of continued relationship, but you need to know how terribly sorry I am for how I hurt you." The language of sin would have cleansed this man deeply and would have freed his niece also. How sad that we missed such an opportunity for healing.

> *The therapeutic systems that I learned in graduate school and in my postdoctoral training do not use a language of sin and therefore do not provide opportunities for confession, brokenness, redemption, and grace.*

I don't sit with my clients and tell them they are a mess, and I don't begin each session with, "Hey, sinner, how are you today?" But I have learned to value a language of sin when I think about the mess we are all in—clients, therapists, and everyone else. And this now plays an important role in how I formulate an understanding of the clinical work I do. If I fail to allow my clients the language of sin,

I risk providing symptom relief while robbing them of the chance to turn around and take the first step on their journey of repentance and change.

➔ PIG SLOP AND THE BATHROOM FLOOR

The language of sin allows us to come to our senses. When Jesus told the story of the hungry prodigal, who looked longingly at the pods he was feeding pigs, the Lord included a powerful phrase in the story: "When he finally came to his senses."[8] The first step of the Christian spiritual journey is coming to our senses, recognizing our sinful and needy state, and heading home toward God's embrace.

> *If I fail to allow my clients the language of sin, I risk providing symptom relief while robbing them of the chance to turn around and take the first step on their journey of repentance and change.*

In each of our lives we have moments of coming to our senses. It may happen while standing in front of a Rembrandt painting, sitting in a therapist's office, participating in a worship service, or praying quietly. Some people come to their senses while scooping pig slop; others are encompassed in the warm embrace of a lover. The moment may start as a gentle nudging, wisps of renewal coming as a gentle summer breeze. Or it may knock us over like a coastal hurricane. We might be alone or sitting in the midst of thousands. So often we find ourselves wandering from home, in a fugue state, drifting away. But in every season and every place God keeps pursuing us, wooing us home, bringing us back to our senses.

Turn us again to yourself, O God.
Make your face shine down upon us.
Only then will we be saved.[9]

In the words of this prayer the psalmist is crying out, "Lord, bring us to our senses."

Annie came to her senses while curled in a fetal position in the middle of her bathroom floor. Sobbing with confusion and remorse, she cried out, "I need church!" It was an unlikely moment to come to her senses because her life was better than ever. Having escaped a broken and dysfunctional home, survived a rigorous and legalistic drug-treatment program, and having disentangled herself from a subsequent drug relapse, her life had become quite stable. She enjoyed a happy and healing relationship with her boyfriend, Brian, and she got along well with his daughter. Annie had found a beautiful family, and their life together was good. But intermingled with her happiness was a nagging conviction that living with Brian out of wedlock was wrong. This awareness of sin kept her far from God, though she longed to come home, and it ultimately drove Annie to curl up and cry, face down, between the oak vanity and the yellow porcelain tub.

Turn us again to yourself, O God.
Make your face shine down upon us.
Only then will we be saved.

Here is how Annie describes it now: "You know how the Prodigal Son had that moment in which he came to his senses? In that moment on the bathroom floor I had a profound awareness of my need for God. It felt like that, coming to my senses. I missed Christian community. I felt disconnected from God. I think I was a helpful person in many ways, but I was missing what mattered most. And that hunger for God, which I had been denying for so long, suddenly came into focus."

Annie was reclaiming a language that she had set aside in the turbulence of young adulthood. During her childhood years and throughout her adolescence she had many encounters with God's grace; she experienced God's comforting presence through her parents' traumatic divorce, and she found a centering hope in God's love through difficult adolescent years. Even after falling into the snare of drug addiction, she looked to a faith-based treatment center for rescue. She knew to look to God for help. Though she found many beautiful people and tremendous help in her treatment program, she also found a stifling legalism that disoriented her and ultimately contributed to her wandering far from a language of sin and grace. She relapsed six months after treatment, and she fell hard.

By the time of the Day of the Bathroom Floor, she had climbed out of the drug trap, found Brian—a man who helped her heal through his kindness and love—and was living the life she longed for. Almost. "I still felt an unsatisfied hunger. Having God at the center of my life was important, but I felt so far from God."

Brian and Annie found a church, and Annie checked a box on a weekly attendance card requesting a pastoral visit. A pastor came to their home, and Annie poured out her story of sin: how far she had wandered from God, how she had been living without considering God or what is right, how she was living with Brian outside of marriage, and yet how she loved him with all her heart. She dumped out the story through tears of remorse and then braced herself for the harsh judgment she expected. But the pastor was a man of grace, and he looked at Annie with kind eyes and simply said, "That doesn't really matter. God is still right here. I see how much this hurts you, so you make the decision today. You come back." She did.

Annie came home.

As she looks back now, contemplating that moment of coming to her senses on the bathroom floor, she sees it as a moment when priorities became clear. Why was she crying when her life seemed so good? Because she was curled up in pain at a crossroads, knowing what she might have to give up in coming back to God. Annie saw that she must be willing to give up her relationship with Brian—this man she loved so dearly and who had helped her heal so deeply—in order to be faithful to God. "I remember thinking, as I was crying on the bathroom floor, about this whole life that I had invested myself in: this relationship, this relationship with his daughter. It mattered, but it didn't. What I really needed was God. That's what mattered. And then I needed the faith to realize that whatever else happened, whether it meant I would have to give this up or not, it would be all right. Whatever happened, I knew I just needed to come home."

As often happens when we speak the language of sin, Annie was surprised by grace. She and Brian were married and found their way back to God together. They have since had two children, daily reminders of God's grace. Annie completed her doctorate in clinical psychology, Brian is working toward a social work degree, and together they have a dream of establishing Grace House, a residential drug-treatment ministry, combining responsible psychology with solid Christian theology to create a healing environment for those caught in the grip of addiction.

> *Turn us again to yourself, O God.*
> *Make your face shine down upon us.*
> *Only then will we be saved.*

At the end of our interview I asked Annie how she envisions God when she finally arrives at her eternal home. "Unconditional love. Having children helps me conceptualize what that is like. I picture an experience with God that is embracing. God sees me—every thought, every action, every deed, every undone deed—and just loves me."

→ FOREIGNERS AND NOMADS

The end of the journey is glorious—being home. The beginning of the journey is found in reclaiming the language of sin and admitting our need. The middle of the Christian journey—where most of us live each day—is disquieting. It is characterized by yearning, by limping through this world as strangers and aliens. We are homesick for Eden but living in a broken place instead.[10]

This is not home. You may stroll down the sidewalk on First Street, as you do every day, carefully stepping over the bulges where the cement is fractured by tree roots and colored with moss growing through the cracks. The blurred sound of passing traffic has become routine; so have the startling honks of road-raged drivers. You know to nurse your left knee as you walk because it gets tender if you walk too fast or too far. It's all so familiar, but this is not home.

The sidewalk leads to the local grocery store where you have been a hundred times, or a thousand times (who can keep track?). Inside you pass by rows and rows of shelves stacked high with food. In the back storage room lie extra boxes of Double Stuf Oreos, and in the back of your mind lie thoughts of famished countries with hungry children. The seventies music plays through the overhead speakers, entertaining baby boomers with the hope they might linger and consume a bit more than usual. Soon you are humming along, "You can't please everyone, so you have to please yourself." "If you can't be with the one you love, love the one you're with." "If loving you is wrong, I don't wanna be right." At the checkout stand you encounter the usual stockpile of tabloids and magazines. Elvis is alive, a seventy-pound woman birthed a forty-pound baby, and aliens were spotted on the White House lawn. The newest swimsuit edition is placed strategically at eye level, where a tanned surgically enhanced body reminds you that you are not a 10 and that you should not be content unless you are sleeping with a 10. You trudge discontentedly back over the exposed moss on First Street, back through the front door with squeaky hinges and a rusty doorknob, back to what you call home. This is not home.

We were built for a place without sin: where justice flows freely, divine kindness prevails, bodies no longer decay, goodness is a way of life, love is never selfish, truth overflows, and beauty requires no implants. As familiar as our current surroundings may seem, however acculturated we may have become, this broken world is not our home.

> *As familiar as our current surroundings may seem, however acculturated we may have become, this broken world is not our home.*

But we are heading home. Michael Card expresses this so beautifully in his song, "I Will Bring You Home."

Though you are homeless, though you're alone, I will be your Home.
Whatever's the matter, whatever's been done, I will be your Home.
I will be your Home.
I will be your Home.
In this fearful, fallen place I will be your Home.

When time reaches fullness, when I move my hand,
*   I will bring you Home.*
Home to your own place in a beautiful land,
*   I will bring you Home.*
I will bring you Home.
I will bring you Home.
From this fearful, fallen place I will bring you Home.

I will bring you Home.[11]

The author of the New Testament book known as Hebrews described many heroes of the faith—those who had given up wealth and security to follow the promises of God. There was a commonality for all these pilgrims: they knew they were not yet home. "They agreed that they were no more than foreigners and nomads here on earth. And obviously people who talk like that are looking forward to a country they can call their own. . . . But they were looking for a better place, a heavenly homeland."[12]

One of the great challenges of living is that we so easily fail to see ourselves as foreigners and nomads. We put down roots, hoping for the satisfactions of this life to fulfill us. We invest ourselves in a house, marriage, career, good health, possessions, friendship, education, children, or ministry—looking for something that will meet our search for significance. But as good as any of these may be, they cannot reach into the hidden corners of our souls and satisfy our deepest longings. These objects of our obsessions keep us scurrying about, distracted from solitude and prayer and wisdom. When we fail to make meaning with the things of this world, we too often end up bitter, angry, cynical, envious, and disappointed with life. Then, perhaps, we turn and blame God, as if all of this is a flaw in the divine plan.

This world is broken. It is not right. This is not the Garden we were created to enjoy. It is only a shattered remnant, an amusement park simulation of real life. Virtual reality. There is no Paradise here—only advertisers trying to sell vacation packages. It need not surprise us that things are a mess everywhere we look. We are foreigners, nomads pitching our tents here and there, but never finding home. We are made for another place.

Richard Foster begins his book *Celebration of Discipline* with these words: "Superficiality is the curse of our age. . . . The desperate need today is not for a greater number of intelligent people, or gifted people, but for deep people."[13] How do we become deep people? Throughout Augustine's *Confessions*, written sixteen centuries ago, he demonstrated a sort of godly yearning that makes the heart grow deep. I have cited Augustine's *Confessions* many times in writing this book because he understood how important the language of sin is to the one who seeks to follow God and how our sin draws us to a place of yearning for home. It is a symptom of our superficial age that we are so often distracted from the task of yearning.

> *We are foreigners, nomads pitching our tents here and there, but never finding home. We are made for another place.*

My family and I enjoy a local Mexican restaurant. We go there for their excellent fajitas, tacos, burritos, or enchiladas. When we sit down at the table, the servers bring tortilla chips. We start eating the chips, one after another, until the bowl is empty. And then they bring another bowl, and we keep eating chips. By the time our fajitas or tacos or enchiladas arrive, we're no longer hungry. We didn't come for the chips; we went yearning for an excellent meal. But we satiate ourselves with chips, and the deeper longing is masked with the pleasures of the moment.

How often do we fill our schedules so full with the pleasures and challenges and glittering images of life that we fail to sit and yearn for the very things that our souls were made to seek? We fail to remember that we are nomads and foreigners made for another home. We fill ourselves up with the tortilla chips of life, settling for pleasure at the expense of joy, for productivity at the expense of meaning.

Life so easily becomes a quest to quiet the din of unfulfilled desires, but nothing works completely: not the wild adventures of adolescence, the exhilaration of new friendship, the companionship of marriage, the thrill of having children, the busyness of career, the benevolence of church involvement, the distraction of socializing, the repose of retirement. There are good things to be found in each of these, but none of them ultimately quenches our deepest thirst for God. Each of us longs for what cannot be found in our world. Father Ronald Rolheiser, in his book *The Holy Longing,* writes: "In this life, there is no finished symphony. We are built for the infinite. Our hearts, minds and souls are Grand Canyons without a bottom. Because of that we will, this side of eternity, always be lonely, restless, incomplete."[14]

We are foreigners and nomads, pilgrims on a journey to a better place.

NINE

$\left\{\; \textit{Pilgrims' Plight} \;\right\}$

Those who travel in a foreign land sometimes face difficult and precarious situations. I recall my adventure in Odessa, Ukraine, with Brent Ellens—then a graduate student and now a psychologist. Brent and I taught a pastoral counseling class at two seminaries.

On our first evening in Odessa, after a lengthy plane trip, we decided to go for a stroll through the city. We set out, Hansel and Gretel without bread crumbs. Odessa is an attractive city with lovely parks bordering the edge of the Black Sea. As we followed the scenery around winding sidewalks and across busy roadways, we somehow lost track of our path and wondered if we knew our way back. Dusk settled in, and we knew darkness was right on its trail. We walked faster, trying to retrace our steps. None of the buildings or roads seemed familiar, and the road signs were of little use because neither of us read Russian. We tried to ask for help, but hand motions and English didn't get us very far. God's compass settled behind the western horizon as darkness fell, and fear settled in.

Brent and I began imagining a cold night wandering the streets of Odessa. Then we remembered that Rod and Lydia Gorter, our missionary hosts in Odessa, had given us a note with their address

written in Russian and slipped it in my coat pocket before Brent
and I left on the walk. Rod also had mentioned that any car passing by would be happy to serve as an impromptu taxi for a few
grivna. So after Brent and I waved our arms in the dark, a kind
Ukrainian passerby stopped to help and then consulted with
several locals about how to find the address scribbled on our scrap
of paper. He eventually found his way. Walking through the front
door of the Gorters' apartment, Brent and I had a faint sense of
being home, yet also an awareness of being so very far from home.

We are foreigners here, yearning for heaven, trying to find our
way through alien territory yet surrounded by hints of familiarity
and reminders of goodness. This is our plight as pilgrims, seen
most vividly in the challenges and rewards of close relationships.

✦ WHERE'S WILSON?

From the moment of life's first breath until our last, there is an
organizing principle that guides much of our behavior, thoughts,
feelings, and motives: we want to be in relationship. The first day
of school is about making friends; adolescents obsess about fitting
in; a major task of early adulthood is forming intimate relationships; middle-age adults struggle through defining and redefining
marriages and friendships; older adults look forward to visits from
friends, children, and grandchildren. We are souls made for
connection, longing for God and for one another, reaching out,
pairing up, breaking up, making up, looking for love, grieving
losses, and yearning for friendship. Relationships are the crucible in
which sinfulness and grace are experienced.

> *Relationships are the crucible in which sinfulness and grace are experienced.*

In the movie *Castaway* Chuck
Noland, played by Tom Hanks, is
a Federal Express systems engineer
stranded on an isolated island for
four years. A pilgrim in a foreign

land with no human companion, Noland creates Wilson, a volleyball stained with his own blood, to be his best and only friend.
Wilson goes everywhere with Chuck. At least in Chuck's mind, they
laugh together, cry together, argue, and reconcile. They are buddies.
Desperate for rescue, Chuck builds a raft, perches Wilson in a spot
to look out for ships passing by, and sets out to sea. But while Chuck
is sleeping, the relentless waves knock Wilson from his perch and
carry him away. Chuck awakes, looks around, and utters the words,
"Where's Wilson?" After some frantic and unsuccessful attempts to
save his best friend, he lies on his raft sobbing, crying out, "I'm sorry
Wilson. Wilson, I'm sorry."

When I saw the scene, I was moved to tears. How crazy is that—
a grown man sitting in a crowded theater crying about another
grown man's losing his volleyball? But the story beneath the volleyball touches me deeply. I am reminded how often in life we cry out,
"Where's Wilson or Susan or Jamal or Brenda or Juan—or God?"
Where are they, and why do we sometimes feel so alone?

I suspect it is true for you, as it is for me, that the moments of
greatest agony and struggle in life have been times of relational
loss or even the fear of such a loss. Someone important to you is
gone: the cancer wins the battle, God seems silent, the divorce
is finalized, or the emotional distance between you and another
feels insurmountable. And the converse is true also: The moments
of greatest joy are found in those connections that are much
too poignant to be captured with words. They are moments of
mystery, beyond definition, when everything seems right: times
of marital bliss, of safe and intimate friendship, of mystical union
with God, of falling in love, of belonging to a community.

We are created for relationship. We yearn for connection.

In Thornton Wilder's play *Our Town*, Mrs. Webb reflects,
"People are meant to go through life two by two." With these
ten words she captures the essence of Wilder's play and much of

human history. We are made for relationships, we celebrate when we find them, and we grieve when we lose them. "Two by two" need not be limited to marriage. Those who are contentedly single still long for friendship and companionship. It is our quest throughout life.

One of my single young-adult daughters showed me a greeting card she had received from a friend. It pictures a room of empty chairs, which the caption describes as a convention of well-adjusted men interested in a committed relationship. My daughter hopes this is more parody than reality. This greeting card humorously expressed what most adults (young and old alike) intuitively know: it is difficult to find a partner for the two-by-two walk through life. Meanwhile, those in midlife tell stories of how difficult it is to keep breathing life into their two-by-two walks. Too often, those later in life are left with disappointed expectations and shattered dreams reminding them of the sin-stained journey.

> *The very fabric of human nature cries out for relationship, yet because of sin in our world and in our souls, relationships are difficult.*

Herein is the challenge. The very fabric of human nature cries out for relationship, yet because of sin in our world and in our souls, relationships are difficult. That which brings the greatest reward also holds the greatest challenge.

➔ FACING FAILURE

Because sin ravages our world, every close relationship is a tapestry of success and failure. This is part of the pilgrim's plight. The relationships that are intended to sustain us and bring us joy are stained by selfish desires, past injuries, wounds and memories from other relationships, and our self-protective urges. The closer we are to another person, the more likely we will see one another's failures.

A new psychologist recently told me that if people suddenly stopped having relational crises, he would no longer have a practice. Sadly, he is in no danger of losing his practice because failure is part of the pilgrim's journey. We may envision a day when relationships are completely pure and good, but that is another day. Today we live in a broken place where we disappoint and misunderstand one another. Relationships have problems, hearts are broken, marriages are splintered, and children are devastated. Failure is part of our close relationships.

> *The relationships that are intended to sustain us and bring us joy are stained by selfish desires, past injuries, wounds and memories from other relationships, and our self-protective urges.*

The story of the Prodigal Son reveals a young man who traded the stability of a loving family for something he anticipated to be more exciting. Maybe he was bored at home, enraged with family members, or maybe his sexual urges drove him away to search for carnal adventure. In the end he had given up everything for nothing. He purchased an illusive dream that left him hungry and alone.

The prodigal's story involves failure, and lots of it, but that is not why we love the story. Failure is the background motif that allows the vivid contours of a bigger story to leap off Rembrandt's canvas. It is an account of the redeeming power of relationship. It is a story of repentance, confession, and forgiveness.

I have witnessed the cleansing power of confession and the healing work of forgiveness many times in my years as a psychologist. Each time I am deeply moved by the simple beauty of this rhythm; it resonates with some unnamed primordial cadence in the human soul. But this is no easy task. Many times—perhaps most times—people cannot do it. The pain is too great, the confession too shallow, or the forgiveness too much to expect. Those who are able to confess and forgive are often called beyond the limits of what they thought possible, yet the healing that ensues takes my breath away: expressions of remorse, tears of loss and joy, and a beautiful dance of humility.

Failure, confession, and forgiveness are not limited to the cataclysmic tragedies of life. We have many opportunities to practice this rhythm of healing as minor failures clutter our daily routines. If it were not for the gift of forgiveness, they would eventually accumulate into a mountain of bitterness and resentment. Living in grace means continually forgiving one another just as God has forgiven us: "You must make allowance for each other's faults and forgive the person who offends you. Remember, the Lord forgave you, so you must forgive others."[1]

Not long ago I borrowed my wife's car for a trip to the lumber store. It didn't go so well. I walked in the back door long-faced, and she immediately noticed my discouragement.

"What's wrong?" she asked.

"I broke your windshield, and I got a ticket."

Then Lisa did what I knew she would do. She hugged me, assured me it would be all right, told me she was sorry for what I had gone through, and offered to make me a grilled cheese sandwich for lunch—with pickles in the middle, just the way I like it. It was a mini prodigal story. The foolish husband comes home to his wife's embrace.

This is a safe example—one that makes me look humble without revealing the messy parts of my life—but things have been much messier. There was the time Lisa miscarried Emma, our unborn child, and in my selfishness I failed to see Lisa's pain or walk with her through the grieving process. My distance added to her pain. There was the time when Lisa told me my expressiveness and warmth with a woman friend was uncomfortable for her and might ultimately be confusing for my friend and me. I dismissed her concerns, confident that I knew what I was doing and that these were simply the neurotic warnings of an insecure woman. Lisa was right, but I deflected blame onto her instead of listening to her valid concerns. At some point I woke up to the reality that I was emotionally entangled with my friend and needed to turn my heart back to my lifelong partner. Lisa has embraced me despite my many failures; I knew she would take a broken windshield in stride. We have walked two by two for many years now, through various failures, challenges, and misunderstandings. These are part of every sinner's love story.

Sadly, in our pride we often fail to see our failures. Psychologists speak of defense mechanisms—the psychological armor we use to protect ourselves from the harsh edge of truth.[2] Our most powerful defenses often come in the context of relationships. Two friends have a conflict, and the first response is for each to conclude, "I am right and you are wrong." The world is neatly bifurcated into two categories: my view (the right one) and your view (the wrong one). It may help us cope with the power of the emotions we are feeling at the time, but our simple division of the world is rarely correct. If conflict continues, our frustrations may end up spilling over onto innocent bystanders—coworkers, children, spouse, the family pet, or strangers on the freeway. Emotional frustrations are displaced and end up hurting those who may be nearby. Or perhaps we project our own failures onto the other, applying labels such as "selfish" or "arrogant." Jesus was addressing our defense mechanisms in the context of relationships when he taught, "First get rid of the log from your own eye; then perhaps you will see well enough to deal with the speck in your friend's eye."[3]

I wonder what my wife's response to the cracked windshield and the traffic citation would have been if I had walked in the door from the lumber store announcing, "I can't believe how lousy Toyota windshields are! I applied a little pressure to fit the lumber in, and the thing just cracked like an eggshell." Or what if I had said, "The police in this town are so petty! He didn't have to give me a ticket, but he must have had a quota to fill." Or maybe I could have figured out some way to blame Lisa for my problems. If I had been defensive or aggressive, I might have received a less gracious response from Lisa.

Herein lie two fundamental principles of human behavior. First, we are prone to defend ourselves rather than humbly admit our failure. During the thirty-minute drive home I sorted through possible ways that this wasn't my fault: the windshield was defective, the employees at the lumber store should have helped load my merchandise and warned me of what I was about to do, or maybe they just build Toyotas too short. It had to be someone else's responsibility. Of course all these explanations failed, and I was left in a temporary state of humility with my failed defenses scattered about me. Humility invites mercy.

Second, we react defensively when others are defensive, so ill will multiplies itself like a virus. If I get angry at you, you are likely to become angry with me. If I defend myself by blaming you for something, you are likely to defend yourself by making it clear that I am to blame. The more I defend myself, the more you defend yourself, and the more you defend yourself, the more I defend myself. A negative cycle is born, and we find ourselves surrounded, entrapped, and infected by the virus of defensive relationships—at home, at work, in our communities, in our political and ideological divisions, and in the wars of the world.

Defensiveness begets defensiveness. Our sinful state keeps us spiraling in a downward cycle, centrifugal forces pushing us further and further apart. We end up blind to our own failure and disappointed in the other's.

⤳ DISAPPOINTED AND DISILLUSIONED

As we wander through this wilderness, eagerly awaiting the Promised Land, we are prone to disappointment in relationships. Others will fail us, betray us, and wound us deeply. We are disappointed in our own failures also. Relationships that begin as wonder and magic sometimes erode to sadness and disillusionment. Marriages wither, friendships fade, children wander, parents die, and God seems distant. This is part of the pilgrim's plight.

We are disappointed and disillusioned for two reasons, one nobler than the other. One is a collective disappointment that points to a future day when things will be right; this is a holy disappointment that enlivens the soul as we yearn for deliverance. The other is a throbbing, disquieting, often demanding disappointment about the way things are; this is a disappointment that despairs of change and wearies the human soul.

Holy Disappointment

We groan in holy disappointment, along with all creation, for things to be made right. I do not mean groaning in a critical sense, as might be the case with whining or complaining, but as a simultaneous utterance of sadness and expression of hope for another day. When my daughter's eighteen-year-old friend died of a brain tumor, we gathered for his memorial service as a community of disappointed groaners, simultaneously speaking our sadness, disbelief, and anger over such a terrible loss and yet eagerly hoping for a day when cancer no longer triumphs over human life. We groan from the uncontrollable discomfort that is an inevitable part of our sinful world, and in joyous anticipation of home.

All creation groans—in frustration and in hope—to be set free. Pastor and author Mark Buchanan reflects: "My hope is that we learn to join our groaning, pitch for pitch and rhythm for rhythm, to the groaning of all creation—earth and sky, waterfall and water buffalo, chickadee and katydid, stone and tree—to all things as they wait for the sons of God to be revealed (see Romans 8:22). Groaning is creation's song, the blues of the cosmos, and we're to hum its melody and take up its chorus."[4]

We groan with our bodies, which remind us that we are material creatures, bound in flesh, in relationship with other material creatures. How many of us rise in the morning and feel some physical discomfort within the first few seconds? Joints are stiff, muscles sore, stomachs churning. With each passing year we carry more reminders that our bodies are frail vessels, wearing out, pointed toward physical death. Those we love change, as we ourselves do: hair grays, stature shortens, muscles weaken, and memories falter. We groan in discomfort, longing for the new bodies promised us in our

> Something is desperately wrong with the world, and we groan in discomfort and long for a better day. Holy disappointment is part of our pilgrim journey.

heavenly home. It amuses me to see the warning labels on exercise equipment. Just about every treadmill, stair stepper, and exercise bicycle has a small disclaimer something like this: "Stop exercising if you feel faint, weak, or short of breath." Whoever thought of these warning labels was quite young. I can't imagine spending ten minutes on an exercise machine without feeling faint, weak, and short of breath! At my age, which is not all that old yet, exercise is synonymous with groaning. And yet I keep exercising, trying to push back this freight train called aging.

We groan as we see the pain of the world around us, when innocent children are abused or hunger claims another life, when cancer devours a young body or a soldier's heart is dissected by machine-gun fire. We groan because relationships are more difficult than we anticipated, because we all seem so prone to misunderstanding and selfishness, because anger and improper sexuality and idolatry and greed so easily beset us. Something is desperately wrong with the world, and we groan in discomfort and long for a better day. Holy disappointment is part of our pilgrim journey.

This sort of disappointment and groaning is a reasonable response in a sinful world. Fortunately, other nomads have walked this same spiritual path in centuries past and have provided us ways to discipline our groaning. Spiritual disciplines—such as prayer, solitude, fasting, confession, guidance, and corporate worship—are structured forms of groaning that allow us to make our hearts known to God while simultaneously allowing us to see the wounded heart of God. They are habits of holiness practiced by Christians throughout many centuries. What is prayer if not groaning for release from our sin, groaning to know God better and to be more fully aligned with our Creator's heart? Fasting is a disciplined groaning that reminds us of our desperate need of and gratitude for God's provision and mercy. In corporate worship we groan together. We groan in discomfort as we acknowledge our need for God, and we groan in anticipation as we celebrate God's presence and goodness all around.

In all of our groaning we long to be released from the bondage of sin. "And even we Christians, although we have the Holy Spirit within us as a foretaste of future glory, also groan to be released from pain and suffering. We, too, wait anxiously for that day when God will give us our full rights as his children, including the new bodies he has promised us. Now that we are saved, we eagerly look forward to this freedom. For if you already have something, you don't need to hope for it. But if

> *What is prayer if not groaning for release from our sin, groaning to know God better and to be more fully aligned with our Creator's heart?*

we look forward to something we don't have yet, we must wait patiently and confidently."[5]

We long for home, and in the meantime we groan in holy disappointment.

Self-Absorbed Disappointment

There is a second sort of disappointment, born out of unrealistic expectations of the here and now. Whereas the first sort of disappointment places us in human community, collectively uttering groans of anticipation, the second places us apart from others. I become disappointed because someone I love behaves worse than I do, or worse than I expect. I consider myself the good guy and label someone else the bad guy. "I'm OK, you're a mess." This is the story of the prodigal's older brother as well as the Pharisee praying in the temple, and I fear it is all too common in our churches and homes. It fails to see the complexity of sin, our complicity in the sin of others, and the magnitude of grace we have each received to cover our sin.

Do you ever feel like a pretty good person? I do sometimes. I am usually nice to my students, treat my colleagues fairly, deeply love those in my family, pay my taxes, provide psychological help to pastors in crisis, go to church and tithe. I don't steal, commit adultery, use illegal drugs, or swear. And I floss regularly. Then I remember the religious leader in the temple. He had the same list: "I thank you, God, that I am not a sinner like everyone else, especially like that tax collector over there! For I never cheat, I don't sin, I don't commit adultery, I fast twice a week, and I give you a tenth of my income."[6] This prayer is the formula to self-absorbed disappointment and disillusionment. When we see ourselves as "pretty good," we misunderstand the gravity of sin and our desperate need for grace. We place ourselves above others, become their judges, and give them the power to disappoint us. "If we say we have no sin, we are only fooling ourselves and refusing to accept the truth."[7] Meanwhile the tax collector kneels in the temple, beating his chest and crying out for grace: "O God, be merciful to me, for I am a sinner."

When I reclaim the language of sin, I see a different self. I micromanage, consume more than my share of resources, and harbor bitterness from past losses. I hoard my time and resent others for intruding on it. I am vain and consumed with how others perceive me. I wrestle with my sexuality and have strayed away from Lisa with my eyes and my heart. I am prideful in my heart and my head. I have learned how to pretend to listen without really listening. I have corrected my children when they needed affirmation. I gossip, care more about eating popcorn at the movies than about feeding the hungry, am envious of highly successful men, and overlook the oppressed. I think more about being great than about being good. I act more spiritual than I am. I am a mess—broken in every way—and my only hope is in God's mercy. "But if we confess our sins to him, he is faithful and just to forgive us and to cleanse us from every wrong."[8]

The apostle Paul was a broken person too. He cried out: "I know I am rotten through and through so far as my old sinful nature is concerned. No matter which way I turn, I can't make myself do right. I want to, but I can't. When I want to do good, I don't. And when I try not to do wrong, I do it anyway."[9]

Paul knew where to turn for help in his weakness. He found everything he yearned for in the embrace of God's grace, including the power to live a better life than he could on his own. "So now there is no condemnation for those who belong to Christ Jesus. For the power of the life-giving

> *I am a mess—broken in every way—and my only hope is in God's mercy.*

Spirit has freed you through Christ Jesus from the power of sin that leads to death."[10] We are sinners through and through, but in the strength of grace God lifts us to our feet, draws us away from sinful choices, and grants unspeakable hope. Our stories of sin and grace are not so much about us as about God.

A physicist friend mentioned an analogy in which each of us is like a lightbulb. We naturally compare ourselves to one another: one shines with 50 watts of holiness, while another has only 25 watts. Maybe the most stellar Christians are 200 watts. But all of these comparisons become trite in the presence of the sun. In the face of God, our different levels of piety are puny and meaningless. It makes no sense to compare ourselves with one another because we are all much more alike than we are different.

> Our stories of sin and grace are not so much about us as about God.

Are we disappointed in others? Sure. Just as we are disappointed in ourselves. We are all pilgrims in a foreign land, all of us quite similar, struggling to make things work, yearning for a better time and a better place. And God is always working, drawing back a broken creation to a place of hope and healing that is found in the language of sin and grace. There is no doubt that you and I have been wounded by others. They are sinners, and that need not surprise us. And, though it is harder to recognize, we have each hurt others by our deliberate choices and our unintentional patterns of defensiveness. Once we see the truth—that we all face faults and struggles—then we can join together in human community without trying to compute who is better or worse. We can cast our gaze on the One who forgives perfectly, redeems us constantly, and embraces us in arms of compassion and forgiveness.[11]

➔ REPENTANCE AND FORGIVENESS

The language of sin, lived out in relationships, calls us to a language of repentance: acknowledging waywardness, bowing in humble contrition, confessing wrongdoing, turning from sin, and committing ourselves to a different path. Repentance is never easy, but it paves the way for forgiveness. Faced with starvation, loneliness, and misery, the prodigal repented of his wrong and turned to head home. He rehearsed his speech: "Father, I have sinned against both heaven and you." Finally, after years of pride, self-deception, and defensiveness he reached a place of repentance. He turned away from his sin and chose to pursue a better way. The father, in turn, responded with forgiveness. He had every right to ignore his apostate son, to send him back to the pig farm to live out the consequences of sin. But instead the father raced toward the son, embraced him, and granted forgiveness.

Regardless of the time-honored adage, time does not heal all wounds. Time heals *clean* wounds. Soiled wounds fester and infect, leading to bitterness and cynicism, to terrorism and war, to divided marriages and wounded children. "Father, I have sinned against both heaven and you." These words helped clean the wound, as repentance does. These words made healing possible. Perhaps the father had already forgiven his son, working many sleepless nights and sorrowful days to do so. If so, it was an internal sort of forgiveness in which the father chose to release his anger. He could forgive, but he was powerless to bring about reconciliation until the wound was clean.

Social scientists who study forgiveness speak of the importance of repentance and apology. "I'm sorry, I was wrong" are powerful, wound-cleansing words. Our natural, prideful tendencies argue otherwise, telling us this is not really our fault, we have nothing to apologize for, the other person should repent first. And the wound festers. What a gift to have eyes to see ourselves clearly as we stand at the pig's trough, to turn and head toward home, contemplating how to express our sorrow and contrition.

At moments in our lives we wake up and see ourselves as we are. With a surge of insight, a flash of epiphany, we recognize that we are hungry and alone, longing for love, while another waits for us to come home. We wake up to see a spouse who has been more right than wrong, a friend whose concerns have been valid, children reaching out to an absent parent, God whose heart aches for our devotion. We awake to delight in another, drawing close through words of repentance.

> *What a gift to have eyes to see ourselves clearly as we stand at the pig's trough, to turn and head toward home, contemplating how to express our sorrow and contrition.*

Lisa once returned from a speaking engagement, unpacked her suitcase, took my hands in hers across the dining room table, and gently drew me into her state of contrition. During her time away she had awakened to a pattern of demandingness in herself. Though I had complained about it from time to time, she could not see it. But after the conference, she could. As her winsome humility distilled into tears streaming down her face, she repented and told me she wanted to change. It was a moment of awakening for her, a great gift for our marriage, and a catalyst for tremendous growth in Lisa and in our life together. Because of Lisa's humility, I have found myself willing to look more honestly at my faults also and to repent of my failures.

When God awakes us to delight in praise, it is through the language of repentance. Israel's King David—known as a man after God's own heart—reclaimed a profound awareness of his sin after wandering far from God. David repented and God forgave.

When I refused to confess my sin,
  I was weak and miserable,
  and I groaned all day long.
Day and night your hand of discipline was heavy on me.
  My strength evaporated like water in the summer heat.
Finally, I confessed all my sins to you
  and stopped trying to hide them.
I said to myself, "I will confess my rebellion to the Lord."
  And you forgave me! All my guilt is gone.[12]

I waited patiently for the Lord to help me,
  and he turned to me and heard my cry.
He lifted me out of the pit of despair,
  out of the mud and the mire.
He set my feet on solid ground
  and steadied me as I walked along.
He has given me a new song to sing,
  a hymn of praise to our God.[13]

Here we see the beautiful rhythm of contrition, repentance, and forgiveness. Augustine reflected: "So, by a humble piety we return to you; and you cleanse us from our evil habits, and are merciful to the sins of those who confess to you, and hear the groaning of the prisoner, and loose us from the chains which we forged for ourselves."[14]

When we humbly admit our weaknesses and faults to God and to one another, we create the possibility for the intimacy we long for and we catch a glimpse of heaven.

Repentance promotes forgiveness. Just as bodies are capable of healing from injuries, so are relationships. Intuitively we know how healing works: we confront unresolved conflict, express ourselves, listen to others, repent of our wrongdoing, forgive others for theirs, change our ways, and come back together as reconciled partners or friends. One person cleans the wound by repenting, and the other offers forgiveness. This is not merely a psychological tactic for getting close to people; it is a rhythm of healing etched into human character by a Creator who calls us to live better lives than we are inclined to live in our broken state of pride.

We may not always receive the forgiveness we hope for from fellow pilgrims; others are broken too, and the damage of sin may seem insurmountable. But we create the possibility of deep human connection by seeing our sin and reaching out in humility to one another. Researchers find that those capable of forgiving have moral humility, an ability to see that they themselves are capable of doing wrong. They may not have done the same things as their offenders, but they recognize in themselves a capacity for sin and are therefore willing to extend mercy to another. Those who have encountered the radiant light of God's forgiveness recognize there is not that much difference between a 100-watt bulb and a 20-watt bulb. We have been shown such amazing grace, how could we withhold forgiveness from another?

My colleagues and I studied forgiveness by listening to the stories of those who had forgiven others. A woman in ministry, deeply hurt by a coworker in the same ministry, reflected on her choice to forgive. "Well, the more I was able to recognize my own failings in situations, the easier it was to forgive. . . . I realized how weak I really am. And when you realize your own humanness in most situations, it's easier to be forgiving of others. You realize they're trying to struggle in their own way. It's all relationships. There's nothing else left in faith but our relationships. To have

> *We have been shown such amazing grace, how could we withhold forgiveness from another?*

broken relationships between you and another person is something you can feel in your prayer life. It comes between you and God."[15]

Humility is the posture of forgiveness, allowing us to see ourselves in those who offend us, to offer mercy instead of punishment, to acknowledge that we are all noble ruins, and to draw together in human community. One man, formerly a vocal opponent of human forgiveness until he was deeply convicted of his own sin and wounded by the sin of another, put it this way: "William Blake says something about heaven, that what we will do is stand around forgiving one another, and in some ways I feel like that is part of what I am trying to learn. Forgiveness has to be the air that I breathe. It has to be a constant thing between forgiving myself and forgiving other people. . . . So I guess I have come a long way from saying forgiveness is not what we are supposed to be doing in this life to saying forgiveness is what we are supposed to be doing all the time."[16]

> *Humility is the posture of forgiveness, allowing us to see ourselves in those who offend us, to offer mercy instead of punishment, to acknowledge that we are all noble ruins, and to draw together in human community.*

Repentance and forgiveness are what we are supposed to be doing all the time. This is the rhythm of a pilgrim's life. Beneath our busy routines and distractions and clutter, we have a spiritual yearning to reconcile with one another and ultimately with God. We long to look beyond ourselves and reach out for love.

✦ GLIMPSES OF LOVE

The life of a pilgrim involves yearning for connection, facing our failures, dealing with disappointment, repenting, as well as granting and receiving forgiveness. This is the language of sin and grace, and when we speak this language, we catch glimpses of love. The power of the story of the Prodigal Son, and of Rembrandt's painting, is in restored love. We don't read the story and say, "Oh good, at least he will have something to eat now." No, we are choked up by the beauty of love. That which was shattered by selfish ambition is now redeemed by the repentance of the son and the gracious response of a loving father. As the father and son embrace, so our disappointments with strained relationships embrace the possibility of forgiveness and healing. And we cling to the possibility of love. The end of the Christian journey is found in the embrace of an all-knowing Creator who loves beyond what any word can express. It is a perfect love, the kind the New Testament writer John knew "expels all fear."[17]

> *As the father and son embrace, so our disappointments with strained relationships embrace the possibility of forgiveness and healing.*

In 1917, after a resident in an insane asylum was carried away to his grave, his attendants found words from an eleventh-century Jewish poem scribbled on his wall. The attendants deemed the words to be the psychotic ranting of a crazy man. But Frederick M. Lehman, a pastor by training, recognized the words, paraphrased them, added some of his own, and in 1919 published a hymn that has been sung around the world.

> *The love of God is greater far*
> *Than tongue or pen can ever tell;*
> *It goes beyond the highest star,*
> *And reaches to the lowest hell;*
> *The guilty pair, bowed down with care,*
> *God gave His Son to win;*

His erring child He reconciled,
And pardoned from his sin.

Refrain:
O love of God, how rich and pure!
How measureless and strong!
It shall forevermore endure
The saints' and angels' song.

Could we with ink the ocean fill,
And were the skies of parchment made,
Were every stalk on earth a quill,
And every man a scribe by trade,
To write the love of God above,
Would drain the ocean dry.
Nor could the scroll contain the whole,
Though stretched from sky to sky.

Can you picture yourself as the psychotic one locked away in an insane asylum, surrounded by the brokenness of shattered dreams and confused thoughts, reaching up to find comfort in God's love? If you can, it's because you understand we are all pilgrims here, caught between the grip of sin and the embrace of grace. Sin is huge. It ravages and incarcerates us at every point through life's journey. But when we compare sin to the magnitude of God's love, sin doesn't stand a chance.

A spiritual director once told me that God is not surprised at our sin. God understands that we are pilgrims wandering in a

> Sin is huge. It ravages and incarcerates us at every point through life's journey. But when we compare sin to the magnitude of God's love, sin doesn't stand a chance.

foreign land and that we will stumble and fall. God does not sit above in grim disapproval. Instead, God grieves alongside us. I cried all the way home from that appointment, not so much in sadness for my sinfulness but with joy that God knows us so well and loves us so deeply.

TEN

$$\left\{\; \textit{Embracing Grace} \;\right\}$$

Lisa and I were sitting at the musty, over-the-hill community movie theater on a January evening when we noticed flashlight rays bouncing down the middle aisle. They stopped right next to us as I felt a tap on my right shoulder. Two of our three daughters were looking for us: "Dad, Mom, you guys need to leave. Megan is at the police station." That got our attention. Our eighth-grade daughter, Megan, had always been delightful, and it seemed unimaginable that some terrible thing had taken her to the police station. The unimaginable became palpable in the minutes that followed. Megan had privately ventured, or perhaps stumbled, into the world of shoplifting. Thankfully, she wasn't very good and was caught early in her aspiring career. The police arrived, cuffed her, took her to the police station, and called our home, where her older sisters took the call and began the quest of finding their parents at the discount movie theater.

We found Megan's repentant and shamed ruins huddled on a wooden bench inside the police station. We talked to the police officer—a good-hearted man who knew exactly how to handle such things—and then left for our silent drive home. Megan walked in the house and went straight to her room to contemplate her shame and her plight. Lisa and I talked for a bit, trying to make sense out of one of the biggest surprises of our lives, and then I went upstairs to say a few words to Megan before bed.

When I got there, words just didn't seem right. So I sat. Megan sat. No words—just silence that seemed too poignant to interrupt with sound. We sat a long time. When I finally got up to leave, I said, "Megan, we will need to talk about consequences tomorrow, after Mom and I have discussed this some more, but for now I was wondering if we could hug." I thought she might resist with the angry defiance that comes in the aftermath of shame, but there was no resistance at all. She stood and clung to me tightly—perhaps as tightly as I grasped her—and we held each other up in one of the most confusing moments of life. It transformed into one of the most cherished moments of my life as she sensed the safety of my embrace and let her tears loose. The tears erupted in heaving sobs of contrition, sorrow, and repentance. And then mine came too—tears of lament for my periods of absence in her life, of regret for the many darts of criticism I had aimed at Megan over the years, of empathic sorrow for the bitter grief now engulfing her, of uncertainty about what the future would hold, and of profound love for this child of mine. There we stood for a long time, two confused sinners, holding on for Megan's life.

That event changed Megan, as defining moments do. Two years after the shoplifting episode Megan told the story to our church congregation before she was baptized. Megan is a college student now—the kind of young adult that every parent wishes for—and we recognize that awful January evening to be one of the milestones in her development. She has since given both Lisa and me permission to use the story in our speaking and our writing, reflecting the sort of courage that has always been part of Megan's character.

→ THE RIDDLE OF SIN

As I was sitting on the floor of Megan's bedroom in bewildered silence, I was aware of holding back the pressing question: "Why?"

"Why in the world would you do such a thing?" "What were you thinking?" Of course, I wanted to ask all these questions and more, but somehow I sensed more communication in our silence than could ever be accomplished with words. In our silence, with no questions being asked and without ever using the three-letter *s* word, we were speaking the language of sin. The language of sin cannot be translated into other languages or explanations, and when we try, we end up with a superficial substitute.

This is what theologian G. C. Berkouwer refers to as the riddle of sin.[1] We are sinners, and our sin transcends explanations and neat theories. When we ask why, we find ways to justify and blame, defending ourselves and driving others away in the process. If I had asked Megan why she shoplifted, we might have ended up blaming each other or together forming an explanation in which we could blame someone else. Perhaps it was bad parenting, or peer pressure, or the materialism of our society that drove her to do it. It's not that these explanations are wrong—they may be legitimate forces in our daily choices—but when we use them to explain our behavior, we minimize and externalize responsibility and fail to see the ominous power of sin working in our lives.

But it gets worse. It's not just that we fail to capture the essence of sin with external explanations that place blame on others; our internal explanations are not that helpful either. We might conclude, "I'm just a bad person," or "I'm weak-willed," or "I have never learned how to behave properly." These explanations may be partly right, but they fail to capture the aggressive forces of sin in our universe. Sin is internal, but it is also external, and in every way it defies our systems of explanation. "It seems to be a fact of life that when I want to do what is right, I inevitably do what is wrong. I love God's law with all my heart. But there is another law at work within me that is at war with my mind. This law wins the fight and makes me a slave to the sin that is still within me."[2]

Take any explanation of sin—"The devil made me do it," "I am morally weak," "I am a victim of past abuses," "I didn't know what I was doing"—and it will be partly right and mostly wrong. Sin is a riddle, and the laws of sin are bigger than we are.

Do you ever watch the evening news on television and during commercial breaks ponder the riddle of sin? "What would make a woman suffocate her own infant?" "How can that man live with himself after defrauding so many people?" "Why does God allow houses to burn with families trapped inside?" After two minutes of commercials—as the muted Zenith sells us toilet paper, e-business solutions, breakfast cereal, and remedies for baldness—the questions loom as large as ever. And they will tomorrow night, and next week, and in decades to come, when our televisions are holographic images in our living rooms.

The riddle cannot be solved. It is not a logic problem. The truth is that we are sinners.

Because we keep trying to solve the unsolvable—to make sense of that which makes no sense—we end up disappointed and disillusioned in our relationships. We are puzzled and surprised when others sin but find excuses for our own sinfulness. We so easily judge others and excuse ourselves.

We recently decided to keep Chale, the family dog, in the laundry room when we are away from home because she had an intractable habit of spending as much time as her schedule allowed on our living-room sofa. We bought a toddler fence and put it in the doorway that separates our laundry room from the rest of the house. The first night she jumped over the fence and slept on the couch. So I built a twelve-inch

Because we keep trying to solve the unsolvable—to make sense of that which makes no sense—we end up disappointed and disillusioned in our relationships.

block to put under the fence, thereby elevating the height beyond the jumping capabilities of a twelve-year-old dog. I felt good to know I could outsmart the HB (a.k.a., hairy beast). But she maneuvered the block away from the fence and squeezed underneath: two nights in a row on the couch. So then I built trim pieces atop the wood block so it could not be maneuvered. The barrier was now impenetrable. For several days, I taunted Chale whenever I walked by: "I'm smarter than you." Then, when we were out of town, our house sitter e-mailed: "Mark, Chale is smarter than you." The HB had figured out a way to climb my barrier and was again enjoying her nights on the couch. Throughout the process, I felt both annoyed and astonished at Chale's capacity to rebel. She is normally eager to please and does what we tell her. Why, when we are out of sight, does she do whatever she wants even if she knows it is wrong?

And then I remembered. I am a lot like the HB. How often do I push down the fences of life or wriggle under the rules? I am more like my dog than I want to admit. I am a sinner.

➔ HUMAN COMMUNITY: SUPPORT AND SANCTIFICATION

When Megan stood sobbing in my arms, two things allowed us to share a moment of true connection: support and sanctification. These same two principles help all of us draw together in human community. Megan and I found loving support in an embrace of understanding. I was clinging to her not as one who is morally superior but as one who also experiences the grip of sin on my life. She was thinking of her failure in that grocery store while I was thinking of my deficits as a father. Our embrace was not, "I am a better person than you, but I will stoop to love you anyway," as much as it was, "Life is tough, and it's messy—let's hang on for dear life." One attitude is condemning, the other is safe. Somehow

Megan sensed the safety enough to let herself go and be vulnerable in my embrace. I wish that all my moments of fatherhood were characterized by this sort of understanding.

Authentic human community calls us to embrace one another with understanding and an awareness of our mutual vulnerability. It is so much easier, so much more natural, to distance ourselves from those stuck in certain sins by seeing ourselves as different. I label them, say to myself, "I could never do that," and so retain my delusions of being basically upright and moral. Other people anchor the scale so that my sinfulness seems minor or inconsequential. I make them the bad guys so I can be a good guy. And I do it because I fear to face my own vulnerabilities. Human community calls us beyond our fearful self-protection to understand that we are all sinners, all fragile, all susceptible to the lure of sin. Even Jesus—the only sinless one in human history, and therefore the only one with a right to stand in judgment—said to the adulterous woman, "Neither do I [condemn you]."[3]

Perhaps paradoxically, the second principle of human community is that we call one another to higher standards. Jesus said more to the woman caught in adultery: "Neither do I [condemn you]. *Go and sin no more*."[4] As Megan and I embraced, we were not only sharing a moment of mutual understanding about our sinful nature, but we were holding each other up. Her sobs were saying to me, "I want to change. I want to live differently." My quiet tears were saying to Megan, "I want to help you change, and I want to confront my failures as a father too."

Sin has consequences. It is costly. The parent who abuses a child may rupture the bond forever. Those who violate the laws of the land may spend time locked away. Spouses with uncontrolled anger often lose their most cherished relationship. Wild sons spend their inheritances. Shoplifting daughters lose some freedom and trust in the weeks ahead. Critical fathers miss the chance to truly know their children. When Jesus told the story of the Prodigal Son, he did not speak directly of consequences, but at the end the father tells the older brother, "everything I have is yours," implying that the prodigal's inheritance was spent and gone forever.[5] The prodigal was welcomed home, lovingly embraced, but the consequences of his choices lived on. In our heavenly home I imagine we will be freed from all consequences of earthly sin, but here in our fallen world we will always face consequences.

Theologians speak of sanctification: growing up in our spiritual lives to be more like the ones God called us to be. A mark of authentic community is to help one another in sanctification. It is not enough to wallow in our sinfulness together. Together we turn around and move in a better direction. We press on. We move ahead. The apostle Paul put it this way: "No, dear brothers and sisters, I am still not all I should be, but I am focusing all my energies on this one thing: Forgetting the past and looking forward to what lies ahead, I strain to reach the end of the race and receive the prize for which God, through Christ Jesus, is calling us up to heaven."[6]

The language of sin calls us to communities marked by understanding and compassion as well as to standards of excellence that call us to encourage and strengthen one another in the journey toward home. Speaking the language of sin calls us to spiritual formation, to a deeper life of devotion to God.

So we have two principles of human community: support and sanctification. But notice the order. Loving support is granted first. The prodigal did not come home to a written contract of consequences

> *The language of sin calls us to communities marked by understanding and compassion as well as to standards of excellence that call us to encourage and strengthen one another in the journey toward home.*

followed by an embrace. The embrace and the party came first: "For your brother was dead and has come back to life! He was lost, but now he is found!" When the Pharisees brought the adulterous woman to Jesus he did not speak first of sanctification and then express mercy. It was the other way around: "Neither do I [condemn you]. Go and sin no more." When Megan and I were hugging, we both knew the time would come to discuss consequences. But that was another time. This was a moment to embrace.

→ INTO THE ARMS OF GRACE

My moment with Megan was powerful, one of the most poignant experiences I have had in my twenty-two years of parenting, and it serves a helpful metaphor for the language of sin and grace that I have discussed throughout this book. But here is the end of the road. The metaphor breaks down for the rest of the story. You see, I was embracing Megan as a fellow pilgrim. Though I am her father and needed to take a leadership role in her life in the days that followed, at that moment we were just two sinners, father and daughter feeling scared and overwhelmed, longing for something better. I was embracing a daughter who made a bad choice but who is overall a very pleasant person. Megan has always been respectful, spiritually minded, good-hearted, and caring. She is easy to love.

In the story of the Prodigal Son the father represents God. This was not an embrace of mutuality, where father and son were both seeing the error of their ways. This was a father who has no error. And this was no easy-to-love son. He trampled on his father's advice and dignity, wasted his inheritance on prostitutes and wild living, and came home with nothing to offer other than a rehearsed line about working as his father's servant. He was an unlovable mess.

This was the whole point of the parable Jesus told. He was

responding to the Pharisees' questions about why he was hanging out and even having meals with despicable people. Why did Jesus have anything to do with the unlovable, messed-up people of his day? The answer to the Pharisees' question is the great mystery of the cosmos. Jesus—God incarnate—loves us. Brennan Manning, author of *The Ragamuffin Gospel,* writes: "He is not moody or capricious; he knows no seasons of change. He has a single relentless stance toward us: he loves us."[7]

God loves us, regardless of how we have failed. God loves us when others don't. God loves us when we despise ourselves. God loves us when we defiantly choose our own foolish path, when we squander our souls with terrible decisions, and when we are lost and far away. God loves us in every season and every place. God loves us, not because of what we are or are not, but because God is love. James Bryan Smith, a spiritual leader and author, writes: "The pain that we have caused through our sin is sometimes staggering and shocking. For years we may have run from God, afraid of his judgment and certain punishment. Off in the distance God stands alone, with a heart broken because we fail to accept his offer of forgiveness. He loves us with a furious passion. He forgives us even when we cannot forgive ourselves. Sometimes I can only sit and wonder at the thought of how much God loves us."[8]

> God loves us, not because of what we are or are not, but because God is love.

Those who seem unlovable in our human perspective are dearly loved by God. What a mystery: God loves the unlovable. There is no other explanation for the lavish grace of the father on his ragamuffin prodigal. The promise of grace—flowing from a heart of love—drew the prodigal from a faraway land, across the arid desert, into the arms of his father. That same heart of love calls to each of us day after day, wooing us away from our distant land of sin, drawing us home to God's embrace. Brennan Manning writes: "Sin has a far greater grip on our hearts and lives than we imagine. And God, who knows this full well, loves us far more than we can imagine, and longs to bring us into deeper, more joyful, passionate fellowship with Himself."[9]

> *When we set the two side by side—our heavy, weighty, monumental sin on one side of the balance, and the depth of God's love on the other side—the side of the scale holding love pounds resolutely on the foundations of the world and resounds throughout all ages.*

When we set the two side by side—our heavy, weighty, monumental sin on one side of the balance, and the depth of God's love on the other side—the side of the scale holding love pounds resolutely on the foundations of the world and resounds throughout all ages. There is no greater force in the universe than God's unfailing love.

My time with the Rembrandt painting at the Hermitage Museum in St. Petersburg, Russia, provided a glimpse of God's love. It was a moment, set apart from the regular routines of life, when God's love began to come into focus. For a moment I was beholding grace. The song has been reverberating in my mind ever since.

O to grace how great a debtor
Daily I'm constrained to be!
Let Thy goodness, like a fetter,
Bind my wandering heart to Thee.
Prone to wander, Lord, I feel it,
Prone to leave the God I love;

Here's my heart, O take and seal it;
Seal it for Thy courts above.[10]

Someday we will be Home, prodigals nestled safely in the arms of a gracious God.

NOTES

CHAPTER 1: MOMENTS

[1] Common grace is a theological term for God's goodness that is available to all humans, regardless of their beliefs or eternal destiny.

[2] Henri J. M. Nouwen, *The Return of the Prodigal Son* (New York: Image, 1992), 93.

[3] If you would like to take a virtual tour of the Rembrandt Room of the Hermitage, visit this Web site: <http://www.hermitagemuseum.org/html_En/08/hm88_0.html>, then click on the links for the Virtual Visit, the First Floor, and number 44 for the Rembrandt Room. Unfortunately the virtual tour does not show *The Return of the Prodigal Son*, but a link at the bottom of the page will lead you to an enlarged image of the painting as well as a description of the work.

[4] The story of the Prodigal Son is recorded in Luke 15, and the story of the tax collector and the self-righteous religious leader is recorded three chapters later in Luke 18.

[5] Luke 18:11-12.

[6] Luke 18:13.

[7] Stanza of "Come, Thou Fount of Every Blessing," words by Robert Robinson (1758), music by John Wyeth (1813). Public domain.

CHAPTER 2: PRELUDE TO GRACE

[1] Barbara Brown Taylor, *Speaking of Sin: The Lost Language of Salvation* (Boston: Cowley, 2000), 41.

[2] Luke 15:18-19.

[3] Colossians 2:23–3:2.

[4] John 8:7.

[5] John 8:11.

[6] Dietrich Bonhoeffer, *The Cost of Discipleship*, rev. ed. (New York: Macmillan, 1959), 45–46.

[7] Isaiah 6:5.

[8] G. C. Berkouwer, *Studies in Dogmatics: Sin* (Grand Rapids: Eerdmans, 1971), 235.

[9] For more on this, see Berkouwer, *Studies in Dogmatics,* 202.

[10] Henri J. M. Nouwen, *The Return of the Prodigal Son* (New York: Image, 1992), 36.

[11] Some readers will remember Thomas A. Harris's 1974 book about transactional analysis, *I'm OK—You're OK* (New York: BBS, 1999).

[12] Jonathan Edwards, *Religious Affections: A Christian's Character before God,* trans. James M. Houston (Minneapolis: Bethany, 1996), 5–6.

[13] Henri J. M. Nouwen, *A Cry for Mercy: Prayers from the Genesee* (New York: Image, 1981), 127.

CHAPTER 3: GRACE AND THE CONFESSION OF SIN

[1] Luke 15:19.

[2] Luke 15:24.

[3] John Calvin, *Institutes of the Christian Religion,* trans. Henry Beveridge (Grand Rapids: Eerdmans, 1997), 38.

[4] These are known as the three enemies of the soul. See Simon Chan, *Spiritual Theology: A Systematic Study of the Christian Life* (Downers Grove, Ill.: InterVarsity, 1998), 63–72.

[5] Henri J. M. Nouwen, *Life of the Beloved: Spiritual Living in a Secular World* (New York: Crossroad, 1992), 73.

[6] A prominent theory in social psychology is called *exchange theory.* The premise is that relationships thrive when both partners contribute as much as they receive.

[7] Romans 5:7-8.

[8] Ephesians 1:7.

[9] I am grateful to Walter Elwell for helping me understand the distinction between sinfulness, sin, and the consequences of sin.

[10] Psalm 51:5.

[11] Augustine, *The Confessions of St. Augustine,* trans. Hal M. Helms (Brewster, Mass.: Paraclete, 1986), 7.

[12] Alvin Plantinga, *Warranted Christian Belief* (New York: Oxford University Press, 2000), 267.

[13] Millard J. Erickson, *Christian Theology* (Grand Rapids: Baker, 1985), 564.

[14] J. I. Packer, *Concise Theology: A Guide to Historic Christian Beliefs* (Wheaton, Ill.: Tyndale, 1993), 83.

[15] Donald G. Bloesch, *Essentials of Evangelical Theology: God, Authority, and Salvation,* volume 1 (Peabody, Mass.: Prince, 1978), 93.

[16] Romans 3:23-24.

[17] The Ten Commandments are found in Exodus 20, and the Sermon on the Mount is found in Matthew 5–7.

[18] Nouwen, *Life of the Beloved,* 73.

[19] Plantinga, *Warranted Christian Belief,* 207.

[20] June Price Tangney, "Moral Affect: The Good, the Bad, and the Ugly," *Journal of Personality and Social Psychology* 61 (1991): 598–607. See also June Price Tangney and Ronda L. Dearing, *Shame and Guilt* (New York: Guilford, 2002).

[21] Richard J. Foster, in his foreword to James Bryan Smith, *Embracing the Love of God: The Path and Promise of Christian Life* (San Francisco: HarperSanFrancisco, 1995), xiv.

CHAPTER 4: SIN AND THE PROMISE OF GRACE

[1] Luke 15:17.

[2] Luke 15:16.

[3] Victor Hugo, *Les Miserables,* trans. Charles E. Wilbour (New York: Knopf, 1997). The part of the story included here is from pages 80–119.

⁴ 1 Corinthians 13:12.

⁵ 1 John 4:8.

⁶ Cornelius Plantinga Jr., *Not the Way It's Supposed to Be: A Breviary of Sin* (Grand Rapids: Eerdmans, 1995).

⁷ Romans 8:20-22.

⁸ This, as described in an earlier paragraph, is the Pelagian view.

⁹ Augustine, *The Confessions of St. Augustine,* trans. Hal M. Helms (Brewster, Mass.: Paraclete, 1986), 21.

¹⁰ James Bryan Smith, *Embracing the Love of God: The Path and Promise of Christian Life* (San Francisco: HarperSanFrancisco, 1995), 36.

¹¹ Henri J. M. Nouwen, *A Cry for Mercy: Prayers from the Genesee* (New York: Image, 1981), 49.

CHAPTER 5: DISORDERED PASSIONS

¹ For statistics of other countries, see statistics on the Web site of the World Bank Group: <http://www.worldbank.org/data/databytopic/GNIPC.pdf>.

² Some of these statistics come from D. Stanley Eitzen and Maxine Baca Zinn, *Social Problems,* 9th ed. (Boston: Allyn and Bacon, 2003).

³ The notion of sin ricocheting is from Cornelius Plantinga Jr., *Not the Way It's Supposed to Be: A Breviary of Sin* (Grand Rapids: Eerdmans, 1995).

⁴ Matthew 15:19-20.

⁵ See Matthew 5:8, 22:37; Mark 11:23; and Luke 24:32.

⁶ See Matthew 13:15, 6:21, and 5:28.

⁷ See Matthew 22:37-40.

⁸ Richard J. Foster, *Celebration of Discipline: The Path to Spiritual Growth* (San Francisco: HarperCollins, 1988) and Dallas Willard, *The Spirit of the Disciplines* (San Francisco: HarperCollins, 1988).

⁹ Alvin Plantinga, *Warranted Christian Belief* (New York: Oxford University Press, 2000), 208.

¹⁰ John Cassian warned against pride early in the fifth century, around the same time as Augustine penned that "pride is the beginning of sin" (*The City of God,* trans. Marcus Dods [New York: Random, 2000], 460). Pope Gregory the Great informed the church of the dangers of pride in the late sixth century, and Thomas Aquinas systematized a discussion of pride in the thirteenth century. In the nineteenth century Dutch theologian Andrew Murray described pride as "the root of every sin and evil." More recently Christian apologist Harry Blamires has suggested that "in the Christian moral system the key sin is pride—that perversion of the will by which the self is asserted as the centre of the universe" (*The Christian Mind: How Should a Christian Think?* [Ann Arbor: Servant, 1963], 89).

¹¹ C. S. Lewis, *Mere Christianity,* rev. ed. (New York: Macmillan, 1952), 109.

¹² Luke 15:29-30.

13 Stephen K. Moroney, *The Noetic Effects of Sin: A Historical and Contemporary Exploration of How Sin Affects Our Thinking* (Lanham, Md.: Lexington, 2000).

14 Augustine, *The Confessions of St. Augustine,* trans. Hal M. Helms (Brewster, Mass.: Paraclete, 1986), 38.

15 Romans 12:3.

16 R. L. Berke, as cited in Nicholas Epley and David Dunning, "Feeling 'Holier Than Thou': Are Self-Serving Assessments Produced by Errors in Self- or Social Prediction?" *Journal of Personality and Social Psychology* 79 (2000): 861–75.

17 Augustine, *Confessions,* trans. Helms, 80.

18 Jonathan Edwards, *Religious Affections: A Christian's Character before God,* trans. James M. Houston (Minneapolis: Bethany, 1996), 130.

19 Luke 18:11.

20 Henri J. M. Nouwen, *The Return of the Prodigal Son* (New York: Image, 1992), 69.

21 Edwards, *Religious Affections,* 134.

22 See Brennan Manning, *The Ragamuffin Gospel* (Sisters, Ore.: Multnomah, 2000).

23 Luke 18:13.

24 John 1:1-4.

25 John 1:14.

26 Philippians 2:5-8.

27 This brief summary of Barth, and Augustine's words come from G. C. Berkouwer, *Studies in Dogmatics: Sin* (Grand Rapids: Eerdmans, 1971), 278.

28 Blaise Pascal, *Pensees,* trans. A. J. Krailsheimer (New York: Penguin, 1966), 42.

29 Edwards, *Religious Affections,* 134.

30 The lyrics are taken from the hymn "Amazing Grace," written by John Newton, later to become part of his collection published as *The Olney Hymns* (London: W. Oliver, 1779).

31 Bernard Martin, *John Newton: A Biography* (London: Heinemann, 1950), 79.

32 Ibid., 87.

33 Ibid., 107.

34 Ibid., 135.

35 Philippians 1:6

36 These hymns were published, along with many of William Cowper's hymns, as *The Olney Hymns* (London: W. Oliver, 1779).

37 Martin, *John Newton,* 271.

38 Ibid., 312, 314.

39 Ibid., 355.

40 Ibid., 363.

41 See Eugene H. Peterson, *A Long Obedience in the Same Direction: Discipleship in an Instant Society* (Downers Grove, Ill.: InterVarsity, 1980).

42 Christian History Institute, retrieved May 7, 2003; <http://www.gospelcom.net/chi/GLIMPSEF/Glimpses/glmps028.shtml/>.

CHAPTER 6: BLUNTED MINDS

[1] Alvin Plantinga, *Warranted Christian Belief* (New York: Oxford University Press, 2000), 207–8.

[2] Galatians 5:19-21.

[3] R. C. Sproul, *Essential Truths of the Christian Faith* (Wheaton, Ill.: Tyndale, 1992), 146.

[4] Dallas Willard discusses the idea of the gospel of sin management in his book *The Divine Conspiracy: Rediscovering Our Hidden Life in God* (San Francisco: HarperSanFrancisco, 1998).

[5] See Micah 6:8.

[6] G. C. Berkouwer, *Studies in Dogmatics: Sin* (Grand Rapids: Eerdmans, 1971), 154.

[7] For an excellent theological introduction to the noetic effects of sin, see Stephen K. Moroney, *The Noetic Effects of Sin* (Lanham, Mass.: Lexington, 2000).

[8] Ephesians 2:4-8.

[9] Justin Kruger and David Dunning, "Unskilled and Unaware of It: How Difficulties in Recognizing One's Own Incompetence Lead to Inflated Self-Assessments," *Journal of Personality and Social Psychology 77* (1999): 1121–34.

[10] See chapter 10 of Helen Prejean, *Dead Man Walking: An Eyewitness Account of the Death Penalty in the United States* (New York: Random, 1993).

[11] Maurice Possley and Steve Mills, "'There Is No Honorable Way to Kill,' He Says," *Chicago Tribune,* 12 January 2003, sec. 1, p. 1.

[12] See Philippians 2:3.

[13] See Mark McMinn and James Foster, *Christians in the Crossfire: Guarding Your Mind against Manipulation and Self-Deception* (Newberg, Ore.: Barclay, 1990).

[14] Dr. Daniel Kahneman, a Princeton University psychology professor and winner of the 2002 Nobel Prize for his research in cognitive errors, won the prize in the field of economics. Findings from cognitive psychology have profound implications in economics.

[15] Though I concentrate on the framing effect in this section, other types of thinking errors abound in the cognitive-psychology research literature.

[16] Although this is generally true, there are exceptions. Social psychologists refer to *Groupthink* as a situation in which a group comes to a false and premature decision and then fails to hear any other perspective. Some members of the group unknowingly serve to guard the group from other viewpoints, and those who dare to speak an opposing opinion are quickly silenced and ostracized. Another exception is when entire cultures are blind to their evil ways, such as the views of slavery prevalent in John Newton's time (discussed in the previous chapter).

CHAPTER 7: NOBLE RUINS

[1] Augustine, *The City of God,* trans. Marcus Dods (New York: Random, 2000), 850.

[2] Zechariah's prayer, found in Luke 1:78-79.

[3] See Karl Menninger, *Whatever Became of Sin?* (New York: Hawthorn, 1973) and O. Hobart Mowrer, "'Sin,' the Lesser of Two Evils," *American Psychologist* 15 (1960): 303.

[4] Philip G. Monroe, "Exploring Clients' Personal Sin in the Therapeutic Context: Theological Perspectives on a Case Study of Self-Deceit," *Care for the Soul: Exploring the Interface of Psychology and Theology,* ed. Mark R. McMinn and Timothy R. Phillips (Downers Grove, Ill.: InterVarsity, 2001), 203–4.

[5] Harry Blamires, *The Christian Mind: How Should a Christian Think?* (Ann Arbor: Servant, 1963), 156.

[6] Ethologists study instinctual behavior in animals.

[7] Isaiah 55:2.

[8] For an interesting and sometimes provocative look at attachment and addiction see Gerald G. May, *Addiction and Grace: Love and Spirituality in the Healing of Addictions.* (San Francisco: HarperSanFrancisco, 1988).

[9] Henri J. M. Nouwen, *A Cry for Mercy: Prayers from the Genesee* (New York: Image, 1981), 24.

[10] Saint John of the Cross, *The Collected Works of St. John of the Cross,* trans. K. Kavanaugh and O. Rodriguez (Washington, D. C.: Institute of Carmelite Studies, 1991), 132. For more on this, see Nicholas C. Howard, Mark R. McMinn, Leslie D. Bissell, Sally R. Faries, and Jeffrey B. VanMeter, "Spiritual Directors and Clinical Psychologists: A Comparison of Mental Health and Spiritual Values," *Journal of Psychology and Theology* 28 (2000): 308–20.

[11] Ephesians 3:18-19.

[12] Henri J. M. Nouwen, *The Return of the Prodigal Son* (New York: Image, 1992), 49.

CHAPTER 8: HOMEWARD BOUND

[1] 2 Corinthians 4:17.

[2] Mark Buchanan, *Things Unseen: Living in Light of Forever* (Sisters, Ore.: Multnomah, 2002), 11.

[3] John 3:16-17.

[4] Roy Hession, *The Calvary Road,* rev. ed. (Fort Washington, Pa.: Christian Literature Crusade, 1995), 21.

[5] Henri J. M. Nouwen, *Life of the Beloved: Spiritual Living in a Secular World* (New York: Crossroad, 1992), 69.

[6] Barbara Brown Taylor, *Speaking of Sin: The Lost Language of Salvation* (Boston: Cowley, 2000).

[7] Henri J. M. Nouwen, *A Cry for Mercy: Prayers from the Genesee* (New York: Image, 1981), 49.

[8] Luke 15:17.

[9] Psalm 80:3, 7, and 19. The psalmist repeats the same prayer three times. In most of our lives we see this theme repeating: we drift away, then come to our senses.

[10] The phrase *homesick for Eden* is borrowed from Gary W. Moon's fine book *Homesick for Eden: A Soul's Journey to Joy* (Ann Arbor: Servant, 1997).

[11] Michael Card (words and music), "I Will Bring You Home," *The Ancient Faith* sound recording (Brentwood, Tenn.: Sparrow Corporation, 1993). Used by permission of EMI Christian Music Group.

[12] Hebrews 11:13-16.

[13] Richard J. Foster, *Celebration of Discipline: The Path to Spiritual Growth,* 3rd ed. (San Francisco: HarperCollins, 1988), 1.

[14] Ronald Rolheiser, *The Holy Longing: The Search for a Christian Spirituality* (New York: Doubleday, 1999), 157.

CHAPTER 9: PILGRIMS' PLIGHT

[1] Colossians 3:13.

[2] For a thoughtful Christian evaluation of defense mechanisms, see Eric L. Johnson's "Protecting One's Soul: A Christian Inquiry into Defensive Activity," *Journal of Psychology and Theology* 28 (2000): 175–89.

[3] Matthew 7:5.

[4] Mark Buchanan, *Things Unseen: Living in Light of Forever* (Sisters, Ore.: Multnomah, 2002), 10–11.

[5] Romans 8:23-25.

[6] Luke 18:11-12.

[7] 1 John 1:8.

[8] 1 John 1:9.

[9] Romans 7:18-19.

[10] Romans 8:1-2.

[11] There has been a great deal of social science research on the topic of forgiveness in the past decade. One of the most robust findings is that people who empathize with their offenders are more able to forgive than others. By seeing ourselves as part of a broken human community, all struggling with sin, forgiveness becomes possible. When we set ourselves above others, as if we are better than they are, then forgiveness is unlikely and difficult.

[12] Psalm 32:3-5.

[13] Psalm 40:1-3.

[14] Augustine, *The Confessions of St. Augustine,* trans. Hal M. Helms (Brewster, Mass.: Paraclete, 1986), 44.

[15] This quote comes from interview research on how people forgive. For more information, see Mark R. McMinn, et al., "Forgiveness Motives among Evangelical Christians: Implications for Christian Marriage and Family Therapists," *Marriage and Family: A Christian Journal* 2 (1999): 189–99.

[16] Ibid., 198.

[17] 1 John 4:18. For a beautiful description of how John experienced the love of Jesus, see Richard J. Foster, *Streams of Living Water: Celebrating the Great Traditions of the Christian Faith* (San Francisco: HarperSanFrancisco, 1998), 32–41.

CHAPTER 10: EMBRACING GRACE

[1] G. C. Berkouwer, *Studies in Dogmatics: Sin* (Grand Rapids: Eerdmans, 1971), 130–48.

[2] Romans 7:21-23.

[3] John 8:11.

[4] Ibid., emphasis added.

[5] Luke 15:31.

[6] Philippians 3:13-14.

[7] Brennan Manning, *The Ragamuffin Gospel* (Sisters, Ore.: Multnomah, 2000), 22.

[8] James Bryan Smith, *Embracing the Love of God: The Path and Promise of Christian Life* (San Francisco: HarperSanFrancisco, 1995), 75.

[9] Brennan Manning, *Abba's Child: The Cry of the Heart for Intimate Belonging* (Colorado Springs, Colo.: NavPress, 1994), back cover.

[10] Stanza of "Come, Thou Fount of Every Blessing," words by Robert Robinson (1758), music by John Wyeth (1813). Public Domain.

MARK R. MCMINN teaches at Wheaton College, where he is the Dr. Arthur P. Rech and Mrs. Jean May Rech Professor of Psychology. He received a Ph.D. in clinical psychology from Vanderbilt University in 1983 before completing postdoctoral training in medical psychology. Mark is a licensed clinical psychologist in Illinois and is board certified in clinical psychology through the American Board of Professional Psychology. His previous books include *Care for the Soul: Exploring the Intersection of Psychology and Theology* (co-edited with Timothy R. Phillips); *Psychology, Theology, and Spirituality in Christian Counseling; Making the Best of Stress; Cognitive Therapy Techniques in Christian Counseling; The Jekyll-Hyde Syndrome;* and *Christians in the Crossfire* (coauthored with James D. Foster).

Mark directs the Center for Church-Psychology Collaboration (CCPC), which functions under the auspices of Wheaton College Doctoral Program in Clinical Psychology. The mission of the CCPC is "Psychology Serving the Church," which it attempts to accomplish through an active research program, training a new generation of Christian psychologists to partner with churches in new and innovative ways, and providing service to church leaders around the world. More information is available through the CCPC Web site: www.churchpsych.org. Mark also maintains a small counseling practice for clergy and their families.

Mark and his wife, Lisa—a sociologist, also on the Wheaton College faculty—live in Winfield, Illinois, and have three grown daughters. Mark enjoys playing basketball, home construction projects, and taking long walks with Lisa.